The Boeing 247
The First Modern
Commercial Airplane

The
Flying Classics
SERIES

Other Books in the Flying Classics Series

The Boeing 247
The First Modern Commercial Airplane

HENRY M. HOLDEN

TAB BOOKS
Blue Ridge Summit, PA

FIRST EDITION
FIRST PRINTING

© 1991 by TAB Books.
TAB Books is a division of McGraw-Hill, Inc.

Library of Congress Cataloging-in-Publication Data

Holden, Henry M.(data)
    The Boeing 247 : the first modern commercial airplane / by Henry
M. holden.
      p.   cm.
    Includes index.
    ISBN 0-8306-3593-9
    1. Boeing 247 (Transport plane)—History. I. Title.
TL686.B65H65 1991
629.133′340423—dc20   91-2618
                                                 CIP

TAB Books offers software for sale. For information and a catalog, please contact
TAB Software Department, Blue Ridge Summit, PA 17294-0850.

Acquisitions Editor: Jeff Worsinger
Book Editor: Suzanne L. Cheatle
Production: Katherine G. Brown
Series Design: Jaclyn J. Boone

Contents

7 The airmail crisis   III

8 The London-Melbourne race   125

9 Boeing in commercial service   133

10 The legacy of the Boeing   149

I have tried to make the men around me feel as I do, that we are embarked as pioneers upon a new science and industry in which our problems are so new and unusual that it behooves no one to dismiss any novel idea with the statement that "it can't be done." Our job is to keep everlastingly at research and experiment, to adapt our laboratories to production as soon as practicable, to let no new improvement in flying and flying equipment pass us by."

William E. Boeing
1929

Acknowledgments

The preparation of this book was not by any means a one-person undertaking, but the combined efforts of many people. Not much has been published on the Boeing 247 and, as a result, material was difficult to come by. One person contributed generously of her time and knowledge to help me create this work. Marilyn Phipps of the Boeing Company Archives appreciated the magnitude of this work and its importance to American aviation history. When all the research avenues I followed led to dead ends, she came to my rescue with Boeing Company documents that had not seen the light of day for more than 50 years. Her uncounted hours of research on my behalf, her help in selecting the right photos, and her skillfulness in substituting photos for those lost to history are together a true measure of her professionalism and dedication to the Boeing Company's history.

Others also helped me along the way: F. Robert van der Linden, Assistant Curator—Aeronautics at the National Air and Space Museum Library, and Larry Wilson and Dave Spencer at the Research Desk, National Air and Space Museum Library.

A special thanks to my research assistant Carole Sandhovel, who made countless telephone calls for me, breaking the ice where it was necessary, and who often was my right and left hands at the word processor. Thanks to Acquisitions' Jeff Worsinger, my editor at TAB Books, for always being supportive. And of course thanks to my family, who puts up with my passion for writing and the moods it brings—my wife, Nancy, and sons Steve and Scott—who were always supportive and encouraging. A special thanks to my son Steve, who during his senior year at Florida State University became my gentle and constructive critic when it came to editing the final draft.

Preface

In 1980 I saw, for the first time, an actual flying Boeing 247. That year the last airworthy Boeing 247 flew into Orlando, Florida, where I was living at the time. Once I climbed aboard this then-aging sky queen, felt its heartbeat, smelled the oil and old leather, I knew I had to find out more about this odd, and old-looking, airplane. What I found out surprised me. Not many people had ever heard of the plane and there was not very much written about it. I decided that either the plane was never worthy of being written about, which was doubtful, or no one had gotten around to it yet. I decided that it must be the forgotten airliner, and perhaps I could do something to correct that injustice.

My plan was to document commercial aviation history between 1925 and 1936—the period I feel contributed most to the commercial aviation system we have today. I was going to begin with the Ford Tri-Motor, progress through the Boeing 247, and wind up the trilogy with the famous Douglas DC-3. Plans don't always work out the way we'd like them to, though, and in this case I am happy to say they didn't. TAB published my DC-3 first, now the Boeing 247 is in print, and I am working on the Ford Tri-Motor.

The fact that my planned sequence has been reversed has given me a new perspective on the history of that period. It is kind of like going in the back door. I was originally going to tie one airplane into the other, showing that the Ford Tri-Motor was really the impetus for the next two. However, as history tells us, that is not necessarily the case. Of course the Ford Tri-Motor got many people thinking about commercial aviation, but the Boeing 247 was in no way the logical successor to the Ford. That, however, is not as clear with the Douglas DC-3, as you will see in chapter 10.

William Boeing did not need the Ford Tri-Motor as the vehicle or the reason to improve the breed. Between the Ford Tri-Motor and the Boeing

...many models, some of which were Williams Boeing's, like the
...All had good points and bad points, and none could keep them-
...the air financially. The Boeing 247 might have proven the viability of
...rcial aviation by earning a profit, but it did not have much time in the
...nt, and it was eclipsed by the Douglas DC-3.
...While it did reign, it had a short but glorious history, and I am proud to
...ne one who tells the story. Only 75 Model 247s were manufactured, and
...day it is no longer flying in the United States. The Boeing 247 left an indeli-
...e mark on the American airline industry and on the world. I hope you
enjoy this history of the Boeing 247, the world's first modern commercial
airliner.

Introduction

The design of an aircraft is not always the deciding factor in its success. Often it is a series of circumstances and the accident of time and place that produces a success. It is usually not the brainstorm of one person either. The basic design of the Boeing 247 airplane combined the technological developments arising at the time with the social and economic needs in the United States over three decades. In the case of the Boeing 247, like most airplane designs, it did not just happen. The circumstances were right for it all to come together.

The Boeing Company made major contributions to the science of aeronautics in those early days. Boeing pioneered the use of electrically welded steel airplane construction. It produced the first successful oleo shock absorbers for landing gear tail skids, wheels, and arresting gears. It produced the first underslung inclined core radiators and reel-type ammunition installation for fixed guns, which eliminated kinking of ammunition during maneuvers. Its greatest contribution to early aviation, however, had to be the Boeing 247. It set the pace for airline design for almost two decades afterward.

The Boeing 247 was a difficult plane for William Boeing to create. It was a complete break from previous conservative aeronautical engineering design concepts and represented a new breed of transport plane, with which earlier types were not able to compete.

To understand how this plane came to be, you must go back to the beginning of the Boeing Company. Between 1916, when Boeing started building airplanes, and 1925, his company concentrated primarily on military planes. With the passage of the Kelly Bill in 1925, which authorized airmail flights by private operators, the Boeing company found itself in an advantageous position since military pursuit planes had much in common with mailplanes. The Kelly Bill changed the Boeing Company drastically, as it would commercial aviation in general.

The Boeing 247's commercial life span was less than 10 years. It did not make a lot of money for Boeing and it was quickly overshadowed by what it had created. Progress waits for no man.

William Boeing's formula for success was rooted solidly in the belief that right answers were to be found only in the facts. For three decades the wall of his outer office bore a placard which read:

2329 years ago Hippocrates said:
1. There is no authority except facts.
2. Facts are obtained by accurate observation.
3. Deductions are to be made only from facts.
Experience has proved the truth of these rules.

That philosophy, as you will see, was the root of the Boeing success.

The Boeing Company today is certainly not the Boeing Airplane Company of 1916. Times, technology, and political perspective have caused the company to grow from 21 people to a work force of thousands. Yet today, the Boeing name is still not compromised.

This is the story of the man—William Edward Boeing—his company, and his model 247. It is an American success story and an illustration of free enterprise at work.

About the author

Henry M. Holden has been a manager in the Network Engineering Departmentment of the New York Telephone Company for 29 years. He holds a B.A. degree in political science from Queens College in New York. Henry is a private pilot and a member of the American Aviation Historical Society and the Aviation Hall of Fame of New Jersey. He is also a member of TIGHAR, The International Group for Historic Aircraft Recovery, and the Aviation/Space Writers Association. He has written more than 200 magazine and newspaper articles.

1

The beginning
1881 – 1918

Today when you fly on a commercial airliner, your chances are good that it will be a Boeing-made jet. It might be an aging Boeing 707, the ubiquitous 727, the diminutive 737, the jumbo 747, or the most advanced airplane in the sky—the Boeing 767 (Fig. 1-1). You enter a warm cabin and take your place in a comfortable, but narrow, seat. The flight attendant will ask you to fasten your seat belt, keep your seat back upright, and tell you what to do if the cabin loses pressure at 35,000 feet. It all seems boring and almost routine to many people. Did you ever wonder where it all began? The name *Boeing* didn't appear overnight, even though more than one generation of Americans associated it with military aircraft.

In the middle of the nineteenth century, a young man named Wilhelm Boeing left Germany for the United States. Like many immigrants he had intentions of becoming rich here in America. Airplanes were unheard of, and only a few "crazy" people talked about the possibilities of a man flying like the birds.

Wilhelm Boeing did fulfill his dream of becoming rich. He settled in Michigan and bought and sold pine forests and iron-ore properties from his Detroit office. When he died he left vast holdings of timber and iron ore in Minnesota's Mesabi Range.[1]

Wilhelm Boeing left another legacy when he died. It was not a name among the corporate giants emerging in America, nor was it that of a multi-millionaire. It was his only son, William, born on October 1, 1881. The elder

---

1. Harold Mansfield, *Vision: A Saga of the Sky* (New York: Duell, Sloan & Pearce 1956), 9.

1-1 The Boeing 767, the most advanced commercial airplane in the world.

Boeing made sure his son had the tools he needed to succeed. Young William had the best education from American and Swiss institutions, including Yale.

Boeing's father died when he was 8 years old. When his mother, Marie Ortman Boeing, remarried, William did not hit it off well with his new stepfather. When he turned 21, he was in his junior year at Yale, and he felt it was time to leave the nest—permanently. With ample funds in his pocket, he decided to follow his father's footsteps. He said goodbye to his mother and stepfather in Detroit and headed west to make his fortune in Washington spruce, just as his father had in Michigan pine. Later he said simply, "I felt the time was right to acquire new timber."[2]

The tall, mustached Boeing had penetrating eyes behind thin-rimmed glasses, and he could have been mistaken for a college professor (Fig. 1-2). Within two years Boeing had a flourishing business, and by 1908 he had moved to Seattle.

In later years some people compared William Boeing to another aviation pioneer, Howard Hughes. They had some common ground. Boeing, like Hughes, was wealthy, aloof, and calculating. He also had a passion for speed and motorized vehicles.

---

2. Reynolds Phillips, "William Boeing," *Boeing Magazine* (November 1956), 4.

1-2 William E. Boeing.

Young capitalists emerging in the early part of the twentieth century were sometimes called "sportsmen" since they didn't keep regular hours like ordinary working people and often enjoyed fast horses or cars. Boeing fit this mold perfectly since he also enjoyed fast cars and yachts. Although some thought Boeing aloof, his friends knew him as a modest, quiet person who seldom gave interviews. Boeing's mother raised him in strict European fashion, and she developed in him a strong need for independence. It was this independence that many people interpreted as aloofness.

Marie Boeing had considerable wealth of her own and a rare business acumen. She was a perfectionist and had a sense of value that later showed up in her son, and in everything he did.

Aircraft construction

The fledgling airplane's popularity spread slowly across the country. Its popularity, however, was not as a vehicle of transportation or even as a potential military application. There were some who argued for its use as a military weapon, but the enthusiasm for the airplane was really for the sensational thing it did. It could carry a person into the sky and return him to the ground safely, at least most of the time.

This ability had people awestruck, especially since the early airplanes were not much more than powered gliders whose aerodynamics were limited to the imaginations of its designers. The available power sources were unreliable and penalized the aircraft in the weight-per-horsepower ratio. If the early designers had closely studied the birds they were trying to mimic, they would have seen the bird's ability to change the overall surface of their wings and flight-control surfaces according to their speed. Today that principle is found in all aircraft, but the undersized control surfaces of early flying machines were better suited to fast planes. As a result, many pilots paid the ultimate price to fly these unstable machines.

Boeing of course had read of man's real and fictional attempts to fly. The mythological stories of Icarus and the Germanic Valkyries amused him, just as Superman and Batman amused later generations. He studied da Vinci's sketches from the sixteenth century and decided they were more fantasy than anything else. He had read of the Montgolfier brothers' first successful balloon flight, but it didn't impress him. Neither did the Wright brothers' victories over gravity convince him that man would or should fly. In fact, the official skepticism of the event ever happening and the Wright brothers' cloak of secrecy added considerable doubt in Boeing's mind. A group of people in the Wright brothers' hometown of Dayton even formed a club, called "The Man Can't Fly Club."[3]

In January 1904, the Wright brothers attempted to clarify the misinformation about their airplane and the Kitty Hawk flight, but the gesture had little effect. Accurate stories by acquaintances and people at Kitty Hawk on December 17, 1903, were, surprisingly, ignored. For the next five years, the Wrights' achievement remained virtually unknown, and many accounts were badly garbled.

Years later, Orville Wright commented on this puzzling reluctance of the American public to believe in airplanes. "I think it was mainly due to the fact that human flight was generally looked upon as an impossibility, and that scarcely anyone believed in it until he actually saw it with his own eyes."[4]

Early progress

In 1909, French airman Louis Bleroit had made the first successful crossing of the English Channel. By 1910, American newspaper writer Harriet Quimby had become the first American to pilot a plane across the 25-mile channel, but within a year she and 37 other American pilots had died in air crashes (Figs. 1-3 and 1-4).[5]

---

3. George Vecsey, *Getting Off the Ground* (New York: E.P. Hutton, 1979), 4.
4. Roger Bilstein, *Flight in America 1900-1983* (Baltimore, Md.: Johns Hopkins University Press 1984), 15.
5. Ibid.

1-3 This 1911 monoplane, built by Louis and Harry Johnson, was the state of the art for the era.

1-4 A 1909 Boland Tailless Biplane. H.V. Pat Reilly, Aviation Hall of Fame of New Jersey

In 1910, someone in Congress introduced a bill to consider airmail operations. The *New York Telegraph* found the idea preposterous. "Love letters will be carried in a rose-pink airplane steered with Cupid's wings and operated by perfumed gasoline" was its patronizing and sarcastic reply.[6]

6. Ibid, p. 17.

What did impress Boeing about man's attempts at flight was Louis Paulhan's spectacular display of airmanship at the January 1910 International Air Meet held at the Dominquez Ranch south of Los Angeles. Paulhan continually defied the laws of gravity by flying the 1.6-mile circular course 47 times.

Boeing decided he had to try this new motorized vehicle himself, or at least have a ride in one. He approached Paulhan and asked if the aviator would take him for a ride. Paulhan said he would gladly oblige but asked if Boeing could come back the next day. Boeing agreed; it gave him another day to watch America's first international aviation event.

The next day Paulhan had another excuse to deny Boeing a ride. Two more days went by, each with a promise from Paulhan that the next day would be the day he would take Boeing up in his flying machine. On the fourth day, Boeing found that Paulhan had left for another aviation event.

Bill Boeing left for Seattle disappointed but silent about his letdown. He learned much later that Paulhan also departed in less than a winning mood. Paulhan was on his way to a court date to defend himself against a Wright brothers' suit. Paulhan was using an aileron device that the Wrights claimed was a violation of their patent. The court upheld the Wright brothers, and Paulhan went back to France to build airplanes without ailerons.

Boeing's first partner

One day while Boeing was sitting in Seattle's University Club, a friend introduced him to an Annapolis graduate engineer named Conrad Westervelt (Fig. 1-5). Both Westervelt and Boeing shared a love for sailing and struck up a friendship immediately. Both were bachelors, and Boeing had studied engineering at Sheffield Scientific School at Yale. They cruised on Boeing's yacht, played bridge, and talked about sailing and engineering. Westervelt would later codesign the first plane to fly the Atlantic (the NC-4) and organize the first commercial airline in China. For the present, however, he was one of the Navy's most outspoken proponents of naval aviation.

Boeing was an avid sailor and none of the boats on the market suited him from a performance or a quality standpoint. To remedy that, he decided to buy the Heath boatyard south of Seattle, on the Duwamish River. This way he could build a boat to his specifications. He had the money, so why should he have to settle for another person's inadequate design?

Boeing and Westervelt sailed Puget Sound regularly, discussing hulls, powerplants, and new designs. Westervelt focused on powerplants and hulls with wings on them. Boeing just listened.

It was an idea that required a good deal of thought. Some people were beginning to accept landplanes as a new technological development of the

I-5 Conrad Westervelt.

The Boeing Company Archives

twentieth century, even though most people did not fly. Flying boats, however—now that was a radical idea. Of course there were men like Glenn Martin building flying boats, but many people thought them unsafe. Silas Christofferson operated a hydroplane service between San Francisco and Oakland, but not many people outside the area had heard of him. Two brothers, Allan and Malcolm Loughead, had a two-passenger seaplane they used to carry passengers to San Francisco World's Fair (they later changed the spelling of their name to *Lockheed*).[7] Boeing had heard a rumor of an airline using flying boats somewhere in Florida. When he read the front page of the *New York Times*, he knew the small St. Petersburg-Tampa Airboat line in Florida was a fact.

Jacques Schneider, the French Undersecretary for Air, set out to improve the reputation of flying boats and flying itself. He created a competi-

---

7. George Vecsey, *Getting Off the Ground* (New York: E.P. Hutton, 1979), 233.

tive event to foster the development of commercial seaplanes. Schneider, the wealthy son of a French armaments manufacturer, loved high-speed boating and became a notable driver of hydroplanes. After meeting Wilbur Wright in 1908, Schneider became obsessed with aviation.

At a banquet following the fourth Gordon Bennett Aviation Cup race for landplanes at Chicago in 1912, Schneider announced *La Coupe d'Aviation Maritime Jacques Schneider*. This annual competition would encourage the development of practical aircraft capable of operating reliably from open sea, with good payload and reasonable range.[8]

The Schneider Cup became a coveted prize in worldwide aviation. The intense competition between the U.S. services in the early 1920s produced a team of American Navy pilots who won the trophy in 1923 flying a pair of Curtiss CR-3 floatplanes to first and second place.[9] Boeing would never win a Schneider Trophy, but his designs would win bigger prizes.

Westervelt's constant talk about flying boats began to eat away at Boeing until he was finally ready to try one. Boeing still remembered an opportunity missed a few years earlier in Los Angeles. On July 4, 1914, Terah Maroney flew a Curtiss hydroplane into Seattle. It caught Boeing's attention and he approached the flyer. When Maroney found out that Boeing had attended the international aviation event in 1910, he befriended Boeing immediately—there were so few aviation enthusiasts in those days. He even offered to take Boeing for a ride. Boeing told Westervelt, "I've been waiting to do this for four years."

The plane today would look like a death trap. The frail "stick and wire" craft was made of bamboo, spruce, and bicycle tubing, and it had two straight wings covered with silk. The craft had a pusher propeller behind the pilot's chair, and the engine hung between the two wings, its radiator nearly touching the pilot's back. Boeing sat alongside the pilot and rested his feet on an open footrest. Boeing adjusted the goggles Maroney had given him and held on with both hands.

The plane bounced down the calm waters of Lake Washington and slowly assumed a shaky resemblance to flight. Boeing could feel the surge of power as the noise of the engine almost blocked out his thoughts. The craft wobbled in the wind and the landscape tilted as Boeing looked down. He could see Westervelt and the others looking up at the plane. They looked small and detached, Boeing thought. After Westervelt had a turn at riding in this new flying machine, the two men decided to try it again. Maroney

---

8. Ron Dick, "The Schneider Trophy," *Air & Space* (June/July 1988): 65.
9. Ibid.

agreed, and Boeing and Westervelt took several more flights in the rickety flying boat.

As they became familiar with the craft, they began to notice that there was not much to its construction. Boeing was sitting on his yacht with Westervelt one day and it came to him. "Why don't we build a flying boat?" Westervelt just looked at Boeing. He knew there was more coming. "We could do it and probably build one better." Westervelt was all for the idea; it might be fun.

"I think one of us should also learn to fly," said Boeing. Since Boeing had financial resources far beyond Westervelt's Navy salary, he would go down to Los Angeles and learn to fly at the Glenn Martin plant. Boeing started out with the same idea many wealthy young men in his day had: to take up flying as a hobby. For several weeks Boeing took lessons with his instructor, Floyd Smith, going up at dawn and dusk when the air was quiet.

Boeing found flying a lot of fun, and before he returned to Seattle he bought a $10,000 Martin seaplane from Glenn Martin, who at the time was the only large airplane manufacturer on the West Coast. The Martin seaplane was also a good example of the most up-to-date American aviation technology.

Boeing considered his friend Westervelt the real engineer of the team, so before Boeing left for Los Angeles he asked Westervelt to collect and analyze the technical data on Maroney's hydroplane. Westervelt agreed.

"I have a friend at MIT [Massachusetts Institute of Technology]" Westervelt said. "I'll write him and ask for some advice." Westervelt was referring to Jerome Hunsaker, also an Annapolis graduate and at the time a leading aviation scholar in the United States. Hunsaker and a young student named Donald Douglas had designed the first wind tunnel in the United States and were using it for aviation research.

Westervelt wrote Hunsaker with questions about the theory of flight, stability, balance, and stress. Hunsaker was glad to send him information.

With the aid of his naval engineering tables, Westervelt studied Maroney's flying boat. After some time, he came to the surprising conclusion that there was no reason Maroney's plane should stay together in flight. "The strength of the parts," he said, "is just about equal to the load they have to carry."[10]

Boeing's first plane: a Martin "TA"

With his flying lessons completed, Boeing returned to Seattle with his seaplane in crates. Boeing had hired a pilot named Herb Munter to assemble the

---

10. Harold Mansfield, *Vision: A Saga of the Sky* (New York: Duell, Sloan & Pearce, 1956), 11.

plane and take it for a test flight. He reported that it just didn't handle right. It stalled in turns, he said.

Boeing, always one to gather and evaluate the facts, decided to find out for himself just what Munter was talking about. Boeing found the plane to be difficult to handle in a turn but even far more unstable while landing. In fact, Boeing crashed, narrowly escaping injury. The crash ripped off the pontoons and the Martin Company said it would be weeks, perhaps even months, before the plane could be repaired.

Boeing and Westervelt decided they could not wait and dismantled the plane to examine its construction. As they laid out the parts on the floor of a boathouse, they began to discover the lack of consistent design in the craft. Some parts that should have been identical were off by inches. The crash itself was probably caused by excessive weight due to the pontoons. The weight and inconsistent construction could easily cause structural failure.[11]

Based on what they discovered from Maroney's plane and what Westervelt had learned from Hunsaker, they knew they could build a better airplane. Boeing decided to fund the construction of two planes. They set up their factory in a small seaplane hanger on Lake Union, about three-fourths mile from the heart of Seattle. Boeing repaired the Martin "TA," put wheels on it, and sold it in 1915.[12]

Boeing had seen the airplane go from the Wright "Flyer" to sturdier-looking vehicles with semienclosed bodies. With that kind of evolution continuing, Boeing could see the day when the airplane would be the world's primary means of transportation. For the present, however, he knew that America was moving closer to a war, and he calculated that airplanes would become an instrument of war. In 1914, the first awkward and ineffectual aerial dogfight and bombing had taken place in Europe. Westervelt had by then convinced Boeing that if you hold the air you can't be beaten, and if you don't hold the air you can't win. The Navy had also opened a small air branch in Pensacola, Florida, and their focus was on flying boats.

Boeing knew America was not prepared for an air war. He saw the rapid advances in Europe made under the pressures of what was then being called "the European war" and was concerned. America did not have airplanes in the same class as Germany's, England's, or France's. If America entered the war, it would pay a heavy price for this unpreparedness. On July 18, 1914, the Army established the Aviation Section within the Signal Corps. The fledgling air service had 6 airplanes, 60 officers, and 260 enlisted personnel.[13]

---

11. Reynolds Phillips, "William Boeing," *Boeing Magazine* (November 1956): 4.

12. John H. Newland, "Reincarnation of 1966," *Boeing Magazine* (July 1966).

13. Roger Bilstein, *Flight In America 1900-1983* (Baltimore, Md.: Johns Hopkins University Press, 1984), 32.

The U.S. government also knew war was coming and the first B&W (for Boeing and Westervelt) was barely on paper when orders came through for Westervelt to report east to Naval headquarters in Washington. Boeing called Dr. Hunsaker at MIT, and Hunsaker recommended a recent MIT graduate engineer named T. Wong to replace Westervelt.

The B&W is born

Since no one in the country had a great deal of aeronautical design experience, Boeing decided that the Martin TA would be a good starting point for his design. He decided his plane should have a larger wing area and lighter construction to correct for the overweight condition of the Martin design, and a larger vertical tail to provide more stability.

The fuselage manufacturing began in the small boathouse on Lake Union where Boeing based his flying activities. The wings and floats were built in the Boeing-owned Heath Shipyards on the tide flats at the south end of Elliott Bay, in Seattle's harbor. The factory workers of the day were skilled carpenters, shipwrights, cabinetmakers, and seamstresses who worked with the spruce lumber, steel wire, and linen fabric materials (Fig. 1-6). Stress calculations and wind tunnel tests were carried out in the MIT wind tunnel in Boston while Boeing and a work force of 21 people completed the two B&W aircraft (Fig. 1-7).[14]

On June 29, 1916, William Boeing made the first test flight of the B&W he called the "Mallard." Not surprisingly, it resembled the Martin plane with a 125-horsepower motor from the Hall-Scott plant in San Francisco. It also had a wingspan of 52 feet—the same as the Martin plane. The top speed of the twin-float plane was 75 miles per hour, and its range was 320 miles. The 27 1/2-foot plane was lighter, however, because it was made from Washington spruce, the lightest wood available to Boeing. The wing section was slightly different because of the precise engineering standards used by Boeing. In an effort to make the machine lighter, wood was routed from the wing spars, the main structural members.

Just before the first flight, and before the wings were covered with Irish linen, Boeing received word from MIT that the wings as designed were too weak. Wong decided to wrap tape around the full length of the hollowed-out wing spars to strengthen them. He then static-tested the wings with sandbags.

The test flight was a complete success and it spurred Boeing to continue. In Boeing's opinion, he had built a better seaplane than Martin, and he could

---

14. TNT network documentary, "Reaching for the Stars."

1-6 Seamstresses are shown sewing linen onto a wing.

1-7 The B&W "Mallard" shown being pushed into the water for its baptism.

do it again. Everyone congratulated themselves on their use of scientific design and analysis.

An interesting fact came to the surface about the B&W 50 years later when the Boeing Company built a replica for its golden anniversary. The spars discovered in the 1916 stress analysis at MIT to be weak due to routing probably were not strengthened by the tape wrapped around them. The tape, the 1966 designers felt, was more of a confidence factor for Boeing and Wong. The 1966 designers also increased the vertical tail area for the same reason Boeing had increased the tail area over the Martin design: more stability.

Herb Munter made the test flight in the second B&W, called the "Bluebill" (Fig. 1-8). He described the seaplane as a "general overcast of a flying machine."[15] The test pilot in the replica 1966 B&W said much the same thing. "It's a big flying machine which in a stiff wind seems to hang in the air while cruising at about 70 miles an hour."[16] The replica, light for its size and with no water rudders (they were not used in 1916), sailed on the water in any breeze, presenting the 1966 pilot with the same challenge of taxiing the craft safely presented to Boeing.

The 1966 replica also had the drag of the original, produced by the inefficient craft. The flat plate drag caused by the engine plus the drag from the struts and wires approximately equalled the total drag produced by another Boeing plane, the 707 jet airliner.[17]

Although in later years Boeing said that he had built the two B&Ws as a hobby, there is evidence to show that he worried about the lack of aeronautical progress in the United States. In 1915, he had formed the Northwest Aero Club to develop aviation interests in Seattle. He had even flown over an indignant group of local pacifists and tossed out missile-shaped cards advocating military preparedness.[18]

Boeing had visions, as did most industrialists in those days, of making a mark on the world. He now had a target in sight. He knew there was a future in aviation and asked his attorneys to draw up a charter to allow his newly formed company to "act as a common carrier of passengers and freight by aerial navigation." Boeing borrowed $60,000 from a bank he owned 75 percent of to organize the company, and he used his personal account in the bank as collateral for the loan.

This would be one reason Boeing made advances throughout aviation's

---

15. John H. Newland, "Reincarnation 1966," *Boeing Magazine* (July 1966): 6.

16. Ibid, 7.

17. Ibid.

18. Reynolds Phillips, "William Boeing," *Boeing Magazine* (November 1956): 4.

1-8 The B&W shown with Herb Munter in the cockpit running up the engine.

early years of development. He was willing to risk his private funds in new ideas, and, like his mother, he was unwilling to accept failure.

Boeing's first company

On July 15, 1916, three trustees—William E. Boeing, president; E.N. Gott, Boeing's cousin, vice president; and J.C. Foley, secretary—approved the charter of the Pacific Aero Products Company.[19]

Boeing sold the two B&W's to the New Zealand government but before he sold them, he flew one for Westervelt.[20] By this time, the B&W partnership had dissolved because of Westervelt's relocation to the East Coast, but Westervelt encouraged Boeing to show the airplane to the Navy.

Knox Martin, the pilot hired by the Navy for the test at $40 a week, took the "Bluebill," the second B&W, up on its first flight on the afternoon of June 29, 1916. The logbook described the weather conditions as a light 15-mile-per-hour breeze and fair skies, and said there was "extreme difficulty in maintaining lateral stability due to unnecessary angle of [the] left wing." In other words, the plane had a leaning for the left. Wong had corrected the problem by the time the plane flew again two hours later.

---

19. Harold Mansfield, *Vision: A Saga of the Sky* (New York: Duell, Sloan & Pearce, 1956), 16.
20. Ibid.

When the two airplanes arrived in New Zealand, "Mallard" went to work for the New Zealand Flying School. "Bluebill," the better flyer of the two, began the first airmail service in New Zealand.

Westervelt was now in charge of all aircraft construction for the Navy, and he encouraged Boeing to design a multipurpose seaplane to meet the Navy's requirements for a Primary Trainer. A modified version of this would be a landplane intended to meet the Army's requirements.[21]

Engineer Wong had some ideas and he had corresponded with Hunsaker. Hunsaker sent some translations of Gustave Eiffel, builder of the famous Paris tower, to Wong. Using some of Eiffel's calculations, Wong developed a revolutionary aeronautical design. He angled the wings and modified the vertical and horizontal stabilizers. European aeronautical designers arrived at the same wing design, called a *dihedral*, about the same time, but with the poor communications existing between the continents, it is fairly certain that Wong arrived at the design independent of European input.

Wong also staggered the top wing over the bottom wing of the biplane to give the airfoil a broader area. Wong even tried his design in a wind tunnel for almost six hours. The plane had a tiny rudder and no stabilizers on the tail, which seemed to bother everyone except Wong. Boeing called the new design, similar to the B&W but with improvements, the Model C.

Herb Munter made the first water test run on November 23, 1916, and reported that the plane needed more rudder area. By January 1917, the Model C was ready for a test flight. Boeing was firm about thoroughly testing it on the water before making any airborne tests. Two more planes were coming off the line and he had to be certain about the plane's performance.

World War I

Events were beginning to happen fast. Between January and March 1917, German "U" boats sunk eight American ships. On April 8, President Woodrow Wilson asked Congress to declare war on Germany. At this point the Aviation Section of the Signal Corps consisted of 55 airplanes (mostly trainers), 35 pilots, and 1,987 enlisted personnel. The Navy and Marine Corps accounted for an additional 54 airplanes.[22]

The next day Boeing gave Munter permission to make the test flight, which was a success. By this time, Westervelt was in the procurement section of the Navy, and Boeing had an inside track. Westervelt urged Boeing to apply for a Navy contract.

---

21. Peter Bowers, *Boeing Aircraft Since 1916*, (New York: Funk and Wagnalls, 1968) 30.
22. Roger Bilstein, *Flight In America 1900-1983*, (Baltimore, Md.: Johns Hopkins University Press, 1984), 33.

1-9 The Model "EA."

Boeing met with his three trustees and they changed the name to the Boeing Airplane Company on April 26, 1917.[23] Boeing then applied for a contract. The Model C easily passed the Navy's tests, and he won a contract to produce 50 trainer aircraft. The two-place open-cockpit trainers were the first of a long line of airplanes built by Boeing for the Unites States government.

Two additional experimental EA models (Fig. 1-9)—landplane versions of the Model C with side-by-side seating and a 90-horsepower Curtiss OX-5 engine—were sold to the Army. The side-by-side seating, the Army found, was a great advantage in a trainer.

In May 1917, the French government asked the United States to furnish 4,500 planes for active service in time for the spring campaign of 1918. To meet this request, as well as the needs of the United States, the Joint Army and Navy Technical Aircraft Board called for 8,075 training planes and 12,400 service planes. The accompanying engine estimate called for 41,810 power plants the first year and 6,159 each month thereafter. All this from an "industry" that only a year before had produced only 411 planes.[24]

23. Peter Bowers, *Boeing Aircraft Since 1916*, (New York: Funk and Wagnalls, 1968), 30.
24. Roger Bilstein, *Flight In America 1900-1983*, (Baltimore, Md.: Johns Hopkins University Press, 1984), 35.

Westervelt had told Boeing the contract was a sure thing, but when Boeing had the signed contract in his hand, he found himself short of help. Wong had resigned, Westervelt was in Washington, and Boeing lacked a formal engineering department.

Boeing used a little ingenuity to solve his problem. He called on the University of Washington and offered them a gift of a wind tunnel if they would establish a course in aeronautical engineering and send him a few promising graduates. The university gladly agreed and sent him several seniors, two of whom would play significant roles in Boeing's present predicament. They also would be a guiding force in the future of the Boeing Airplane Company.

Clairmont Egtvedt (Fig. 1-10) and Philip Gustave Johnson knew nothing about designing airplanes, but they were mechanical engineers. Johnson became a draftsman and Egtvedt's job was to develop stress analysis tables. By the time the war was over, the two men had played a significant role in helping Boeing turn out the 50 Navy trainers.

A year after coming to the company, Egtvedt was named chief experimental engineer and shortly after that, chief engineer. There was, however, one more word in the title than there were people in the department.

1-10   Clairmont Egtvedt.

The Boeing Company Archives

Egtvedt spent 49 years with Boeing and with almost startling rapidity rose through the ranks.

Egtvedt's early interests were far removed from those of the modern aeronautical engineer. His concerns were with the testing of woods, glues, metals, varnishes, gunk, and fabrics.

Egtvedt had hands-on familiarity with his profession that put him in touch with the frail aircraft of those days. With a pad of paper tied to his leg with a rubberband, he would take notes on airspeed, temperature, oil pressure, rate of climb, and altitude-problems—things now dealt with singly by large bodies of specialists working with exotic metals, instruments, and scientific data.

Those were tough, formative years for Boeing, but Egtvedt gathered ideas and experience and rose to vice president – general manager by 1926.

The Navy contract for trainers meant Boeing had to expand. The small factory on Lake Union would no longer do. Boeing decided set up shop in the Heath shipyard he had bought a few years earlier. Most of the existing buildings and equipment were suitable for making wooden aircraft parts. From humble beginnings in less than 6,000 square feet of floor space, the Boeing Airplane Company blossomed to more than 45 different military and commercial models by 1929.[25]

An interesting aspect of Boeing's character was his search for excellence. He was impatient with imperfection. His embarrassment in front of a Navy inspector at Hampton Roads, Virginia, illustrated his sense of pride in his company. The inspector found a frayed aileron cable on a trainer plane and Boeing was furious. He dispatched a telegram to Seattle that read, "A fine state of affairs .... For the good of the company the person responsible has to go. Any such laxity is unpardonable and I for one will close up shop rather than send out work of this kind."[26]

Boeing was also a man of interminable patience. He was willing to sink time and money into a project if he thought he was going in the right direction of progress. He would support the person in spite of temporary failures.

Boeing works for the competition

The war was winding down as the last of the fifty trainers rolled off the line. Victory was in sight and the Navy decided it didn't need any more trainers. The Navy, in its infinite bureaucratic wisdom, then gave Boeing a contract to build 50 Curtiss HS-2L flying boats, the Navy's standard patrol and bomb-carrying flying boat of World War I (Fig. 1-11).

---

25. "America's Aircraft Builders & Their Products, *The Sportsman Pilot* (August 1929): 25.
26. Reynolds Phillips, "William Boeing," *Boeing Magazine* (November 1956): 4.

I-11 The Curtiss HS-2L.

The Curtiss planes were huge flying boats that required Boeing to enlarge his facilities again. Boeing looked upon the order with mixed blessings. He was beginning to get a handle on design work, but the Navy had halted his progress in favor of helping one of his competitors. The brighter side of the coin was that the Boeing Company was making money.

Although not a Boeing design, the HS-2L was an important milestone because it provided not only the incentive but also the design and production experience that were to contribute heavily to the first postwar Boeing Airplane, the B-1 Flying Boat.

Boeing continued to work on his own design ideas, and the Curtiss planes were already coming off the assembly line when the bottom fell out. It was November 11, 1918. The war was over. There was cheering and celebrations in Seattle and all over the world.

The next few months would show the dark side of the victory in Europe, and particularly for the fledgling airplane industry. Within days of the armistice, the government canceled orders for 13,000 aircraft and 20,000 engines. No funds were available for even a small number of new aircraft, and the Navy canceled half of the Boeing-made HS-2L flying boats. From April 1917 to November 1918, American producers had delivered 13,984 planes with the capacity to turn out 21,000 aircraft per year at the time of the armistice. The war's end choked off the lucrative military contracts, and only 780 planes were built in 1919, all but 8 for the military.[27]

Even with the dark clouds of a postwar recession on the horizon, Boeing was optimistic. He believed commercial aviation had a future. Airplanes had grown bigger and engines were more powerful. You did not need a crystal ball to reason that someday airplanes would carry passengers, move freight, dust crops, and fly mail. Boeing began to talk about a commercial plane called the "B-1—B" for Boeing and *1* for the first commercial model.

---

27. Roger Bilstein, *Flight In America 1900-1983*, (Baltimore, Md.: Johns Hopkins University Press, 1984), 7.

Postwar doldrums
1919–1925

When the war ended, Boeing and the other airplane manufacturers knew much more about building airplanes. Government funding had gone a long way to advance the state of the art. After the war, the momentum of invention and enthusiasm subsided and returned to the piecemeal and frustratingly slow development of the prewar industry.

It didn't take long for the postwar recession to hit Boeing's young company. One estimate said over $100 million in government contracts were canceled after the armistice.[1] If it were any consolation to Boeing, the entire industry suffered. The hugh surplus of airplanes and Liberty engines created for the war caused a standstill in the industry. Egtvedt and Johnson went hat in hand to the Army and Navy, trying to secure orders.

One of the orders the Army gave Boeing was to build an armored attack bomber. The three-place open-cockpit triplane marked a bold attempt by the U.S. Army to design a plane that could withstand heavy ground fire. The GA-1 (Fig. 2-1) was built to strafe ground troops and installations. The engine nacelles and fuselage were completely covered with heavy armor plate to withstand head-on fire from the enemy. In the absence of bullet-proof glass, revolving shutters gave the pilot and gunners a blinking view of the target. The machine was powered by two Liberty 12-cylinder engines with pusher-type wooden propellers. There were four machine guns and a 37mm cannon in front, and one machine gun aft.

After the first GA-1 was in the air, the Army gave Boeing a contract to build its successor, the GA-2 (Fig. 2-2). Like the GA-1, the GA-2 was built

---

1. George Vecsey, *Getting Off the Ground* (New York: E.P. Hutton, 1979), 95.

2-1 The Boeing GA-1.

2-2 The Boeing GA-2 was still an awkward and inefficient plane, and not long for the aviation world.

under the postwar policy of the Army designing the airplane and contracting for its manufacture by the aviation industry. The first GA-2 was built exactly as designed by the Army, but the second was built with extensive revisions as a result of Boeing's experience with the 10 GA-1 planes and the first GA-2.

The GA-2 convinced the Army that the armored attack plane concept was not practical, and further development of the type was abandoned.

These planes were capable of heavy loads but lacked the desired flight characteristics. The Army decided in favor of maneuverability and speed.

Boat-building to shore up the Boeing plant

As the recession deepened, even the small orders dried up, and Boeing went back to building boats. When that wasn't enough to pay the bills, he branched out to manufacture sea sleds, bedroom furniture, and armchairs.[2] Boeing even looked into the market potential of Ouija boards. He believed in his company and drained off a large sum of his private resources to keep it together. This action enabled him to pay the bills, though at times just barely, and keep the company together.

To Boeing, no problem was incapable of a solution. "You keep working on it," he said, "and eventually you will find the answer that is right."[3]

Boeing's employees had faith in him, too. In later years, Clair Egtvedt said that he had a substantial sum invested in railroad securities because he believed in the future of transportation. He also invested in aviation, heavily in Boeing stock.

The Boeing stock was literally the product of the sweat of his own brow. Part of his pay in the lean years at Boeing came in the form of stock. "It wasn't always possible to sell it," he said, "so I eventually accumulated quite a bit that way, through stock splits and on the market."[4]

In 1921, the financial situation in the Boeing plant brightened a little. The Army awarded Boeing a contract to produce 200 MB-3As (Fig. 2-3), an improved version of the Thomas-Morse MB-3. This was Boeing's first large airplane order from the Army since World War I, and it started Boeing toward a dominant position in the fighter plane business.

Eddie Hubbard—More than an airplane driver

Eddie Hubbard was the top test pilot in the Boeing organization. Boeing had hired him in 1917 when Hubbard was 28 years old. In experience, Hubbard was an old hand—he had been flying since 1912, part of the time as an Army flight instructor in San Diego.

Hubbard had already made a name for himself in the Air Service when Boeing hired him. On July 4, 1916, Hubbard and Lt. E.T. Condon flew a sack of mail from Seattle's 13th Naval District to the Army's Camp Lewis, near

---

2. TNT network documentary, "Reaching For the Stars."

3. Reynolds Phillips, "William Boeing," *Boeing Magazine* (November 1956): 4.

4. Egtvedt biographical files, Boeing Company.

2-3 MB-3A.

The Boeing Company Archives

Tacoma, about 50 miles away. Their flight was to celebrate Independence Day and show the speed of a modern airplane. They averaged only about 35 miles per hour on the return trip because of headwinds, so it is probably fortunate the flight is largely forgotten.

Hubbard was also the first pilot to conquer the spin. Before Hubbard's daring move, once a pilot went into a spin, there was no way out because of certain self-perpetuating forces of aerodynamics. No matter how a pilot struggled with the controls as the wind screamed through the wires, he was careening toward almost certain death.

Hubbard thought about the aerodynamics of the rickety aircraft and asked, why struggle with the controls? Just center the controls and wait. If the plane is high enough, the wings and natural aerodynamic forces should help the plane recover into normal flight. It was an idea with no empirical information for its foundation. Anyone he talked to about it thought he was crazy.

While he was an Army instructor, Hubbard decided to test his theory. If he were wrong he would probably pay the ultimate price. One day he took an Army plane up and deliberately put the plane into a spin. Fortunately for Hubbard, his theory worked. Neutralizing the controls restored the plane to normal flight. The Army's reward for discovering this life-saving technique was to fire him for jeopardizing their equipment.

One day Hubbard went to Boeing with an idea that would launch Boeing into new horizons. On May 15, 1918, the U.S. Post Office inaugurated air-mail between New York, Philadelphia, and Washington. In the early days, air-mail service was a dangerous and sometimes fatal way for a pilot to earn a living. Of the first 40 airmail pilots, 31 died on the New Jersey – Chicago route, mostly over the foggy Allegheny Mountains.[5]

The airmail routes were dangerous for pilots because of poor weather forecasting, no radio beams, lack of instruments, no lighted airways, and the generally unreliable water-cooled Liberty engine. To make matters worse, the engines were put into fragile and poorly balanced airplanes.

In spite of such alarming statistics, Hubbard saw a hidden potential. The boundaries of the United States limited the government and its routes, and that was where Hubbard saw an untapped potential.

Boeing sent Hubbard to Washington to talk with Post Office officials about a need for airmail service between Seattle, Washington, and Victoria, British Columbia. Hubbard's idea was to pick up the mail that missed the boat out of Seattle and fly it to Victoria, the boat's last stop before it sailed across the Pacific. He would also fly mail from inbound ships back to Seattle. The Post Office could not fly such a route without causing border problems. There was, however, nothing to stop a private citizen from providing this service. This was the kind of commercial venture Boeing was looking for to pull his company out of its financial doldrums.

The Post Office and the Canadian government agreed to give Hubbard's proposal a one-time trial, and opened the route to Boeing and Hubbard on March 3, 1919.

The flight, timed for the opening of the Vancouver Exposition, would focus attention on the event and hopefully demonstrate a practical use for airplanes. At that time, the flight was probably moot since few Americans and Canadians believed the airplane had a commercial future. The flight, which delivered 60 letters to the *Africa Maru*, a ship bound for Japan, got more public attention and coverage in the history books than the inauguration of regular scheduled international airmail service a year later (Fig. 2-4).

The Boeing CL-4S floatplane was a modified Navy trainer, the last one off the production run and built for William Boeing rather than the Navy. It carried serial number 700, so Boeing logically called it C (commercial) 700. After installing a Hall-Scott L-4 engine, it was redesignated CL-4S.

After the successful flight, Boeing considered staying in the airmail business. After discussing it with Ed Gott, his general manager, however, he decided to concentrate on building airplanes. He did, however, encourage Hubbard to bid for the mail contract.

In September 1920, the U.S. Post Office announced that Hubbard had won the contract and agreed to open the mail route to him permanently.

---

5. George Vecsey, *Getting Off the Ground* (New York: E.P. Hutton, 1979): 109.

2-4 Eddie Hubbard (left) and William Boeing with Victoria mailplane (CL-4S).

Boeing leased space in the hangar to Hubbard and made the CL-4S available to him until the B-1 was ready.

Hubbard began daily service flying the 78-mile route on October 15, 1920—the first regular international airmail service.[6] A reporter recorded the inauguration flight. "On a cold, windy and rainy day, a small group of people watched with mild interest the inaugural flight of the Seattle to Vancouver Mail Service. Seattle postmaster, Ed McGrath, proclaimed the historic day ... a day to remember."[7] The reporter sarcastically wrote that he noticed more than a few yawning spectators among the 40 or 50, but he did not explain why anyone should be tired at 2:00 in the afternoon. The paper had a photo of a lonely pilot by a lonely biplane on Lake Union.

---

6. Kenn C. Rust, "Early Airlines" Part 1, *American Aviation Historical Society Journal* (Winter 1985): 261.
7. *Seattle Star*, 15 October 1920.

History has no photographs of the engine warm-up, ribbon cutting, or hand-shaking dignitaries. There are no pictures of the plane taking off or circling over the small crowd. Even the Wright brothers had better coverage at Kitty Hawk. To make matters worse, the return flight was late and landed after dark. Only a single mechanic greeted Hubbard.[8]

The event was so widely forgotten that those who recalled it at all in later years said the event was to mark the first Boeing commercial venture into airplane design, the B-1 flying boat. What is also forgotten is that Hubbard did not use the B-1 on his first, second, third, or even fourth flight.

B-1: The first Boeing commercial venture

In late November 1920, the B-1, the first Boeing airplane designed from scratch by Egtvedt as a practical commercial airplane, was ready for testing (Fig. 2-5).

Some of the hands-on familiarity that Clair Egtvedt was noted for was at best nerve-racking and at worst downright dangerous. One very close call came when he and Eddie Hubbard first flew the Boeing B-1.

Undeterred by someone who offered to bet William Boeing that the plane would never get off the water, Egtvedt and Hubbard taxied the open cockpit flying boat past a long row of ships anchored in Lake Union. Hubbard poured on the power, and the plane rose sharply into the air and up over the anchored ships. Then the engine stalled and the plane started to dive toward the ships. The engine kicked in and they zoomed skyward just over the masts, only to have the whole procedure repeated.

Like a bucking bronco, the plane zoomed and dived until Hubbard found a clear spot and made a hasty landing. Later the "failure analysis" found that the fuel pump only worked when the plane's nose was down; it stopped when pointed up. A modified fuel pump and a wider elevator were the solution. After two additional successful flight tests, Hubbard put the B-1 into regular service on his mail run.[9]

This venture had significant payoffs in addition to the revenue it earned. It gave Boeing an opportunity to show how rugged and dependable his plane was, and it gave Hubbard the unique experience of flying a schedule and maintaining the equipment over months of use. These opportunities would be significant factors in the Boeing Company's development.

The venture also gave Hubbard some unsettling moments. Once, with a full load of mail, he flew into a headwind and ran out of gas. He landed in

8. Hubbard biographical files, NASM.

9. Egtvedt biographical files, Boeing Company.

2-5   The Boeing B-1.

Salmon Bay after dark and drifted for two hours before someone noticed him. He was able to buy some gas and finish the trip, so the mail was brought home safely. The frugal Hubbard later admitted that because of the high cost of Canadian gas, he had tried to nurse his existing supply.

Another time he was in serious physical danger. He had just taken off when a rudder cable snapped. The plane keeled over and crashed in ten feet of water. Witnesses to the crash thought Hubbard was dead. The plane landed upside down and sank quickly. After about a minute, Hubbard popped to the surface holding the two bags of mail. The captain of the ship from which he had just picked up the mail rescued him. The mail and Hubbard finished the trip by train. Hubbard later recovered the plane, repaired it, and put it back into service.[10]

Hubbard received $200 per trip on his mail run. At first the government limited him to 12 trips a month, and he carried about 600 pounds of mail on each trip.[11] The $2,400 each month yielded him a comfortable profit after he paid for fuel, parts, and his one part-time mechanic. Hubbard invested these profits in real estate, bank shares, and Boeing stock. His combined financial interests would soon make him a millionaire.

---

10. Hubbard biographical files, NASM.
11. R.E.G. Davies, *Airliners of the United States Since 1914* (Washington, D.C.: Smithsonian Institution Press, 1982): 46.

The lonely B-1 that chugged up and down the 50-minute route on its seemingly never-ending odyssey saw service from 1920 to 1928. It flew between 25,000 and 50,000 pounds of mail a year.[12] During this time it flew 350,000 miles on the mail route, wore out six engines, and required no important structural changes. When Hubbard retired the Boeing B-1, it was still capable of flight, but its historical value was greater.

The B-1 never found a commercial market for Boeing because of the availability of cheap war-surplus aircraft. Today it is in the Boeing Museum of Flight in Seattle, Washington.

Electric arc welding—A Boeing innovation

Clair Egtvedt was hopping around the country trying to get people interested in Boeing-built planes. He had canvassed the Army and the Navy and had run into a dead end on both attempts. On his way back to Seattle, he stopped off at McCook Field in Dayton, Ohio, to watch the Army train its pursuit pilots. When a pilot came out on the losing end of a landing, he always blamed the plane (if he survived).

Egtvedt met Lieutenant Charles N. Monteith, an engineer and a pilot at McCook (Fig. 2-6). Monteith told Egtvedt the problem was too many cooks in the kitchen. "The equipment branch has the last word on equipment," Monteith said, "and the engine branch has the last word on the power plant, and no one has a common goal." Egtvedt also knew that the good engineers in the Army were all leaving for the private sector, so this might be an opportunity for Boeing.

Monteith continued. "The Army expects us to pursue the enemy, outrun him, outmaneuver him, and outshoot him. We have to be able to turn on his inside, and with these airplanes we can't do that. The brass hangs equipment on them that we never use. We need them stripped for action. These planes are too heavy to be pursuit planes."

That comment had Egtvedt thinking as he traveled back to Seattle on the Pullman. He knew that, in addition to the weight Monteith talked about, the aerodynamics also caused the plane to fly more slowly and to be less maneuverable.

He thought about how tight a pilot dared to turn in a pursuit plane. If his turn was too tight, the bolts holding the wood together pulled apart because of the aerodynamic stress. Then it was goodbye plane and pilot. Metal tubing and arc welding would solve the problem of the plane coming apart under the stress of a tight turn.

---

12. Ibid.

2-6 C.N. Monteith (center).

As the train entered the Rocky Mountains, Egtvedt began sketching drawings of ideas as they popped into his head. When he got back to Seattle, he sat down and showed some of his sketches to Boeing. It was January 1922, the economy was beginning to improve, and Boeing showed an interest.

The real problem Egtvedt saw was that the Army dictated rigid specifications that did not allow a plane manufacturer much leeway. Build it the way the Army wants it, or don't bother building it at all. There was very little incentive and profit if one were to build a pursuit plane the way the Army thought it wanted one built.

The wooden deHavilland DH-4 was originally designed with a two-bladed wooded propeller, ailerons in both wings, and external controls. The Army wanted to modernize its fleet and had Boeing rebuild 187 DH-4s to DH-4Ms, with steel-tubed fuselages. From this order Boeing gained valuable experience in producing metal airplanes. The DH-4M was the first production plane in the United States to have a steel-tubed fuselage.

Boeing had developed a process for electrically arc-welding thin-gauge steel tubing to replace the spruce timbers in his airplanes. This skeleton of hollow metal bones reduced the weight of the plane and prevented it from becoming unglued in the air. It was the success of this welding technique and his aggressive pursuit of government contracts for military planes that would eventually make Boeing one of the largest airplane manufacturers in the country.

Boeing does the unconventional

One day Boeing and Egtvedt sat in the office discussing the Army's rigid rules. "Why don't we take a chance," Boeing said, "and build a pursuit plane to our specifications, then try and sell it to the Army?"

Egtvedt looked at Boeing. "You mean use our own money?"

"No," Boeing said. "We'll use my money." Boeing didn't want to dwell on that point. "We'll be able to build the performance and efficiency we want into this plane. We could make it the best pursuit plane in the world."

Boeing turned from the window that overlooked the Olympic skyline and faced Egtvedt. "I want you to investigate every source you can find. Get all the information on the latest theoretical and practical designs, and after we build it, we'll fly it to Dayton and enter it in competition."

Egtvedt went to the National Advisory Committee on Aeronautics (NACA, the forerunner of NASA) and obtained information on wing sections and data on control and stability. It was far from adequate, so he began examining other airplanes for their shortcomings and making notes not to use those design components.

On his model, he designed a short bottom wing to reduce the number of wires needed between the wings. In the process, this feature also reduced the drag between the wings. Next he relocated the radiator under the engine. He inclined the engine so the radiator would still get the full sweep of the wind in a climb but the "flat plate" resistance in level flight would also be reduced significantly.

Glenn Curtiss—Boeing's nemesis

By July 1923, the plane was ready for the Army competition. The Boeing PW-9 (Fig. 2-7) nosed out the hottest plane at the show, a Curtiss. The Army, however, worked in strange ways. Curtiss won the overall competition and the contract. Boeing won an order for two PW-9s.

There was disappointment in Seattle. Boeing had invested a lot of money in what he thought was a sound idea. In retrospect, he still thought it was. The politics of Washington had played heavily on the Army's decision. After all, Curtiss planes were the Army's favorites. That was not to say Boeing could not displace Curtiss. At the moment, however, he didn't know how he would do so.

Boeing did not let go of the pursuit-plane idea. After a great deal of politicking on the part of Egtvedt, the Army finally agreed to extensive trials of the PW-9. The results were surprising and upset many people in Washington. The Army focused on the Curtiss, but it could not ignore the results of Boeing's PW-9. The Boeing was just as good as the Curtiss, and in some respects, as far as turning ability went, better than the Curtiss. The Army decided to order both types and Boeing got an order for twelve. "Now we're getting somewhere," Egtvedt said.

Two Army officers had just piloted an Army Curtiss PW-8 from Roosevelt Field, Long Island, to San Diego in 26 hours 50 minutes. This feat

2-7 The PW-9.

2-8 The Fairchild Model 71, an early mail/passenger plane.

confirmed Boeing's feelings about the future of aviation. A dozen years earlier it had taken Cal Rogers 49 days to cross the continent in a fragile aircraft called the *VIN FIZ*.

By 1924, the U.S. economy was brightening. The war was becoming a forgotten nightmare and business was picking up. Boeing was still trying to get the Navy's attention and finally did in the spring of 1924, when he won the Navy's competition for training planes. The Navy awarded him a contract for 49 NB-1s and NB-2s (*N* for Navy, *B* for Boeing.).

Simultaneously, the U.S. Post Office announced that it was going to buy an experimental mailplane from each company that wanted to build one to Post Office specifications (Fig. 2-8). The Post Office had finally conceded that the deHavillands, which had carried the mail since 1918, were finally wearing out. Boeing authorized his plant to build a plane based on the NB-1 design. There was one problem, however. The Post Office required the use of a Liberty engine, since the government still had a stockpile of these engines left over from the war.

It was now January 1925, and Boeing made Phil Johnson first vice president, and Clair Egtvedt vice president and chief engineer. Boeing was beginning to think of retirement while he was still young enough to enjoy himself.

3

The birth of United Aircraft & Transport
1925–1930

The federal government played an important role in the development of commercial aviation and the future of the Boeing Airplane Company. In 1910, Congress discussed a bill to determine the feasibility of scheduled airmail service. The bill died before it left the ground. The poorly constructed stick and fabric aircraft had no chance of proving that concept.

After World War I, the Post Office joined with the Army's Signal Corps to test the concept again. By this time, planes were stronger and somewhat more reliable. On May 15, 1918, they inaugurated airmail service between New York and Washington. In the three-month experiment, the Army flew 254 trips covering more than 29,500 miles. The experiment was a success (Fig. 3-1).

The Post Office continued to fly the mails into the early 1920s while beacons and markers were installed on the airways. The routes grew and by 1925, the system stretched across the country. It was now time to offer the routes to private operators through competitive bidding.

The passage of the Kelly Bill (Air Mail Act) on February 2, 1925, was the first step toward serious, planned, commercial air transport. It encouraged commercial aviation by authorizing the Postmaster General to contract with the private sector for airmail service. The Kelly Bill paved the way for William Boeing's venture into commercial air transportation and the privately operated, scheduled airlines of today.

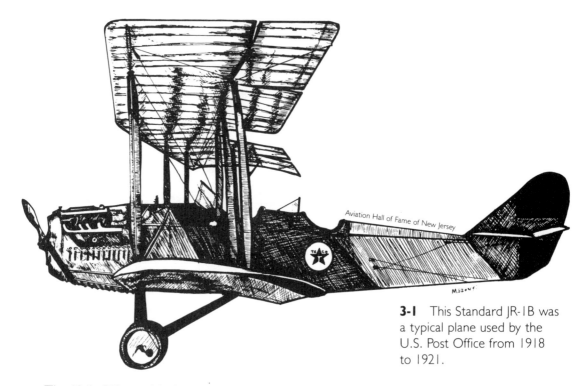

Aviation Hall of Fame of New Jersey

3-1 This Standard JR-1B was a typical plane used by the U.S. Post Office from 1918 to 1921.

The Kelly Bill provided that the low-bid winner would receive up to four-fifths of the postal revenue carried on his aircraft. This was clearly a subsidy, but the government hoped that, by legislating sufficient profit for an operator to pay for his equipment and expenses, privately operated commercial air-lines would expand. Their expansion would encourage the development of larger and better aircraft. Airmail became a windfall for some private com-panies and was very popular with the public. A letter could cross the country in as little as 36 hours, compared to surface mail, which took four to five days.

At the time of the Kelly Bill's passage, Europe was far ahead of the United States, with 18 passenger-mail carriers.[1] In the United States there was only one passenger-mail airline, Pacific Marine Airways, which had been operating in Southern California since late 1920.[2]

The private operators would soon learn that passenger-mail combina-tions were not always profitable. Bad weather, which fouled up schedules, underpowered planes, and lopsided rates soon made them realize that pound for pound, people were more expensive to carry than mail.

---

1. Roger Bilstein, *Flight in America* (Baltimore, Md.: Johns Hopkins University Press, 1984), 52.
2. Kenn C. Rust, "Early Airlines," Part 1, *American Aviation Historical Society Journal* (Winter 1985): 261.

3-2 Stout's first all-metal commercial airplane: the 2-AT, "Maiden Dearborn."

The Kelly Bill gave a shot in the arm to the disorganized and haphazard aviation industry. It encouraged men like Ford into commercial development, but it did not make flying safer, or its reputation better. On the contrary, things grew worse. It also did not deliver the economies needed to allow the industry to operate subsidy-free.

Immediately after passage of the Kelly Bill, things began to happen. On April 13, 1925, the Ford Motor Company became the first authorized private mail carrier under the legislation. The plane used was a single-engine, all-metal monoplane from the Stout All-Metal Airplane Company (Fig. 3-2).

Henry Ford and his Tri-Motor

There are few historical records of Ford's far-reaching aviation efforts, but they have equalled if not surpassed the achievement of the automobile. Ford took the airplane, considered by most people at that time to be a noisy and dangerous machine, and transformed it into a successful commercial product. His product was radically different. His all-metal airplane design, called the *Ford Tri-Motor* and nicknamed the "Tin Goose," hinted at things to come (Fig. 3-3).[3]

There was no field in the 1920s that offered more opportunity to the inventor than aviation. The science of aeronautics was still in its infancy. Apart from actual airplane construction, there were many deficiencies in airplane design that needed to be identified and corrected.

---

3. All Ford literature capitalized and hyphenated the words *Tri-Motor* whereas all other three motored aircraft were described *trimotor*.

Smithsonian Institution

3-3 Stout's first all-metal trimotor bore a close resemblance to the first Ford Tri-Motor. Note the open cockpit above the wing. In 1925, Stout Airlines became part of the Ford Motor Company.

Even before World War I, airplane designers recognized that the boxlike construction of the fabric-covered planes was inherently weak and unstable. To compensate for the lack of strength, they added wires and supporting struts. The wires held the plane together when the aerodynamic forces tried to tear it apart, but they also created additional drag and aerodynamic problems. Nevertheless, wire-and-strut construction became an important part of airplane design. The philosophy was, "the more wires and struts the stronger the plane."

There was a story told that one airplane manufacturer would release a pigeon inside the body of a plane. If the bird could fly out of the plane, there weren't enough wires to hold the plane together.

On August 25, 1925, Ford announced his entry into the commercial aviation field and his goal. "The Ford Motor Company," he said, "means to prove whether commercial flying can be done safely and profitably."[4]

Ford attempted to convince the public that flying a Ford plane was the right thing to do. In August 1925, he established the Ford Air Reliability Tours, covering 13 cities and 1,900 miles. The winner received a cash prize and a trophy.

The event was open to all aircraft manufacturers, and it attracted one of Europe's best-known aviation figures, Dutch-born Anthony Gerhart (Tony) Fokker. At the time, Fokker was building an aircraft plant in New Jersey, and

4. David Ansel Weiss, *Saga of the Tin Goose* (New York: Crown Publishers, 1970).

3-4 This Ford Tri-Motor flew Admiral Byrd over the South Pole, and was the first plane to make the journey over the Pole.

for the race, he converted his newest transport, a single-engine F-VII, to a trimotor. There is speculation that a glimpse at the plans for Ford's Tri-Motor prompted him to do so. The modified Fokker dominated the race, coming in first, and followed three minutes later by the Ford entry, a single-engine "Air Sedan."

Both Ford and Fokker profited enormously from the publicity. Ford bought Fokker's trimotor for Admiral Richard E. Byrd's North Pole Expedition. The publicity Fokker received was enough to launch his trimotors on a successful career in America.

Ford's trimotored aluminum-alloyed behemoth, built as some said like a brick wall, and Fokker's wood-and-fabric trimotor would volley back and forth for popularity and profits. Admiral Byrd's flight over the North Pole in the Fokker trimotor and his subsequent flight over the South Pole in a Ford Tri-Motor (Fig. 3-4) were giant steps toward the public's acceptance of aviation.

Ford used his trimotors to carry auto parts, mail, and executives on the 260-mile trip between his Dearborn factory and his Chicago offices. When the fledgling airlines, such as National Air Transport, saw the Tin Goose, they immediately placed orders for the trimotor (Fig. 3-5).

Although the Ford and Fokker airplanes dominated the commercial aviation network of the '20s, they also had serious design deficiencies and lacked the basic creature comforts (Fig. 3-6). The airplane would still have to demonstrate that it was safe, reliable, and comfortable. This would not be easy, certainly not for the Fords and Fokkers.

There were accidents where the wings fell off the wooden planes in flight. If a Ford had an engine failure on takeoff, the resulting vibrations and

Smithsonian Institution

3-5 Stout's 2-AT, "Maiden Dearborn II," at the Ford Reliability Tour. This plane flew Ford auto parts and personnel between Detroit and Chicago.

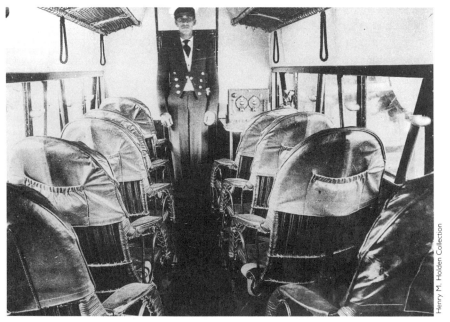

Henry M. Holden Collection

3-6 The interior of a Ford Tri-Motor.

3-7 The foot-thick corrugated wing of a Ford Tri-Motor gave it plenty of lift. Note the external surface control "horns." If ice or snow froze on these horns, disaster followed.

the poor airflow over the corrugated skin would sometimes cause the plane to crash (Fig. 3-7). Engineers had their work cut out for them to solve the technical problems that plagued early aircraft.

The popularity of Ford's plane stemmed from its shape. It was different. It had no wires or struts, and its metal skin had corrugations running with the spans.

Aluminum was stronger than wood and Ford tried to convince the public that his planes were safe and comfortable. An advertisement for the Ford Tri-Motor said, "Your comfort is given the same consideration as the structural strength. The enclosed fuselage has plenty of windows, permitting good visibility and ventilation. Exhaust manifolds throw the sound away from the fuselage, and padding the compartment further muffles it. Conversation is carried on with ease. Large upholstered chairs assure riding ease for twelve passengers."[5]

5. John Neville, "Ford Motor Company and American Aeronautical Development," Part VI, *Aviation Magazine* (September 1, 1929).

This was, at best, a benign overstatement and in no way resembled reality. Although the advertisement spoke of comfort and safety, the sound level inside a Ford was 117 decibels—the same level as a subway train.

D.W. Tomlinson, one-time chief pilot for TWA, had flown hundreds of hours in Ford Tri-Motors. "Flying in the old Fords," he said, "was an ordeal from the passenger standpoint. The flight was deafening. The metal Ford shook so much it was an uncomfortable experience. It surprised me that people would pay the money to ride in the things."[6]

Bailey Oswald, chief designer for Donald Douglas's early DC series, had the same criticism. "I often wondered what a person saw in them. It was almost something a person felt they had to do to prove something. It was a dangerous machine, and safety amounted to almost nothing."[7]

Copilots handed out packs of chewing gum, cotton, and ammonia ampules to passengers. The gum equalized the pressure on the passenger's ears, the cotton blocked out some of the noise, and the ammonia relieved airsickness. Airsickness was so common on the southwestern flights of Transcontinental Air Transport (TAT, later TWA) that someone suggested putting pictures of the Grand Canyon on the bottom of the airsick cups so no one would miss the view.

When passengers arrived at their destination, they got off the Tri-Motor physically and psychologically exhausted. Their bones ached, their nervous systems were a jumble of skinny wires all sounding different notes, and their heads pounded from the constant propeller noise. Aviation technology would have to come up with something better.

The Air Commerce Act: Organizing the airways

Fierce competition existed between the airlines for the few passengers who dared to fly. Those who flew did because they found their businesses could not afford a long train ride. Time was money and they were in a hurry and were willing to endure the primitive accommodations offered by the noisy and dangerous airplanes. An assortment of movie stars found flying another way to gain publicity.

In 1926, Congress passed the Air Commerce Act, which formed the aeronautical branch of the Department of Commerce. This act provided for the licensing of planes and pilots, and the lighting of the airways. It was the foundation for a cohesive plan for the development of commercial aviation. Over the years the government had sunk millions into improving the airways,

6. Nova TV documentary, 17 December 1985.
7. Bailey Oswald interview with author, 25 March 1987.

3-8 The Douglas M-2 mailplane. The U.S. Post Office purchased 51 of these mailplanes in 1926, and Western Air Express used 7 between Los Angeles and Salt Lake City, a route later to become one of William Boeing's links to the transcontinental route. By this time the Douglas Aircraft Company was also using welded steel tubing in the fuselages.

and the results were beginning to show. Between February 2, 1926, and April 4, 1927, airmail pilots logged over 3 million miles without a fatality.[8]

Improved airways was good news for Boeing and the private sector, too. By 1926, there were 12 private contractors flying mail on 14 routes, many with passengers. There was an assortment of equipment, but basically two categories: big planes and small. The big planes, like the Curtiss Carrier Pigeon and the Douglas M-2 mailplane (Fig. 3-8) carried 1,000 pounds of mail at about 120 mph, and used the Liberty engine. The smaller planes, like the Pitcairn Mailwing (Fig. 3-9) and the Stinson SB-1, used the smaller 220-horsepower radial Wright "Whirlwind" engine and carried 600 pounds of mail at about 115 mph.[9]

There was speculation that the airplane companies would build mailplanes that would have mail clerks aboard, just as railway mail cars did, and

8. George Vecsey, *Getting Off the Ground* (New York: E.P. Hutton, 1979): 109.

9. Kenn C. Rust, "Early Airlines," Part 1, *American Aviation Historical Society Journal* (Winter 1985): 270.

3-9 The Pitcairn Mailwing.

that the mailplanes would haul the bulk of their cargo between dusk and dawn. The airplane was becoming faster, and in many cases it eliminated the loss of any business hours in transportation of mail and express between many cities.

Transcontinental airmail—The dawn of a new age

In 1927, Eddie Hubbard came back to a growing Boeing Company. He was now vice president of operations.

Up to this point, Boeing had concentrated his product line on pursuit and attack aircraft. One day an excited Hubbard burst into Clair Egtvedt's office. He had another brainstorm. "Clair," he said, "the Post Office has just laid a golden egg. They're going to put a transcontinental airmail route up for private bids, and the Chicago-to-San Francisco segment is the first piece. This is the opportunity of a lifetime. If we can build some mailplanes, I have the math and mileage to show that we can make money."

Egtvedt did not show much enthusiasm about Hubbard's idea. Without the subsidy, the mail-passenger carriers could not make money. The airplanes were too heavy and the engines too inefficient. A transcontinental route would have additional obstacles to overcome, including bad weather (especially in the winter), and long distances over the rugged Rocky Mountains.

Egtvedt felt that Boeing also lacked the experience. Boeing was almost exclusively a manufacturer of military planes. They had built one mailplane for the U.S. Post Office, an experimental Model 40. The Post Office purchased it as they had agreed but did not follow up with additional orders.

The major problem with the Model 40 was the aging water-cooled Liberty engine. The Post Office insisted the private mailplanes use them to deplete the war-surplus inventory. The engine was heavy, almost 850 pounds dry, and it was now old and showing its age in maintenance problems. The 12-cylinder 450-horsepower engine lasted only 50 hours in the air. Its most notorious failing was it could not hold oil and leaked like a sieve.[10]

Egtvedt's analytical mind sorted through the possibilities. "Why don't we try the new Wasp air-cooled radial engine on the Model 40?" he said. Egtvedt planned on using the new Wasp engine on the Navy's fighter planes he was designing, but it did have other possibilities.

At the time, the Boeing Company accurately reflected the conservative market attitude of aircraft design. Boeing himself was conservative in his policies and engineering, and this attitude was reflected among his officers. They accepted the market requirements of traditional airplanes.

Boeing's later apparent break with tradition would shock the industry. Boeing's progress in the early years came from refining established designs, not innovative thinking. Some innovative designs went down on paper, but that is as far as they went.

Hubbard sat is silence. Egtvedt's idea was daring and meant going against the government's established tradition of using only Liberty engines for mailplanes. Although a 220-horsepower radial engine has been on the scene since the early 1920s, it could not compete with the 420-horsepower water-cooled Liberty engine. Therefore the traditional thinking was a mailplane mated to a Liberty engine.

The Pratt & Whitney 425-horsepower Wasp radial engine weighed 650 pounds—200 pounds less than the Liberty engine—and that meant an additional 200 pounds of mail could be loaded aboard. The increase in payload would make Hubbard's proposal even more attractive, and the low-maintenance prediction was another incentive. Early versions of the Pratt & Whitney Wasp needed an overhaul every 150 hours, three times longer than the Liberty engine, and later models rose to 300-hour intervals in 1929 and reached 500 hours by 1936. By then maintenance costs had dropped 80 per-

10. PBS network documentary, "First Flight Around the World."

cent. These savings represented perhaps the biggest contribution of engine manufacturers to airline development.

"Work up the new figures using the Wasp engine and see what comes off the slide rule. If it looks good," said Egtvedt, "we'll take it to Bill."

Boeing always evaluated all the facts and fit them into a carefully developed picture. Having run a timber company and an aircraft company simultaneously, he had absorbed the details of both businesses. He knew the area the mail route would cover.

Boeing listened to the two men, examined the figures, and then worked up his own set of figures. He compared the two sets of numbers and sat back in thought. After what seemed like an eternity, Boeing spoke.

"I don't like it," he said looking at Hubbard. "This is something new to us. It has a high probability of risk and failure. We would have to risk airplanes, pilots, and a great deal of capital."

Hubbard reminded Boeing that the two of them had flown the mail just a few years earlier.

"That was different," replied Boeing. "We didn't have to deal with blinding snowstorms and the Rocky Mountains."

Hubbard countered with the reminder of the snarling winds he had fought in the Strait of Juan de Fuca on his mail run. It was some of the worst weather in North America.

"There are risks," Egtvedt acknowledged, "but if we don't do it, someone else will."

He was right, Boeing thought. He had been watching the Western Air Express mail routes. Western appeared to be doing well. It completed 90 percent of its scheduled flights with only 38 forced landings. It also had carried 209 passengers on one route at $60 each for a one-way trip, earning a $12,540 profit.[11] With the right kind of operation—one that had sturdy planes, reliable engines, and good management—the venture should be profitable.

Boeing recognized the lesson in the bottom line. In spite of heavy mail loads, a handsome profit could be made from carrying people, if managed properly.

Because of Western's fine record, they attracted more than Boeing's attention. The Guggenheims awarded them a $180,000 grant to develop a "model airway" for passenger services between Los Angeles and San Francisco. This was an extraordinary sum of money in those days. The goal was to prove that an airline could make a profit from passenger revenue alone.[12]

11. Kenn C. Rust, "Early Airlines," Part 1, *American Aviation Historical Society Journal*: (Winter 1985) 264.
12. "Beating the Odds, The First Sixty Years of Western Airlines" (no author) 7.

The Boeing Company Archives

3-10 This was Boeing's Model 40 mailplane, and Boeing's answer to the converted military deHavillands that carried the mail.

It was obvious to more than just Boeing that there was a future in air transportation. Mail routes were regulated by the government, but an airline could take passengers anywhere.

By 1927, ninety percent of the airlines' revenue still came from government postal contracts, which paid by the pound.[13] Some airlines made passengers sign agreements that allowed them to be dumped anywhere along the line if the company needed the room for the more lucrative mail cargo.

Another thought crossed Boeing's mind. A Boeing-run airline might serve as an outlet for the planes he built. The combination of an airplane manufacturer and operator made sense. By pooling their knowledge they would make more progress than a single operator or a single manufacturer would.

Phil Johnson had said, "Efficiency will count much more than it did in the experimental and colorful days of the past. The dominant survivors will be factories and operating companies that are well managed and financed, with designing and manufacturing staffs capable of keeping pace with the changes coming in both the building and operating sides of the industry."[14]

---

13. Robert E. Johnson, *Airway One* (: Lakeside Press, 1974).

14. Philip G. Johnson, "Recent Developments in Air Transport," *Aeronautical Engineering Research*, AER-51-26 (1929).

It wasn't long before Boeing would expand this idea of pooling his resources, but for now, the immediate problem would keep him awake a few nights. There was also the job of convincing the government that it was time to junk the Liberty engine.

Several days later, Boeing reached a decision. The new Wasp engine in a mailplane like the Model 40 (Fig. 3-10) would give him the competitive edge he needed, but there was still another problem. The first 24 Wasp engines were going to Navy fighter planes, and none would be available for commercial use for at least a year. Without the Wasp engine, Boeing would not chance the venture. As coincidence would have it, Phil Johnson, now his vice president and general manager, was in Washington discussing the delivery schedule of the fighter planes with the new Wasp engines. Boeing called and told him to renegotiate the dates. Boeing then took a chance and submitted his bid.

Without knowing it, Boeing made one of those historic and far-reaching decisions, but he was not a gambler and did not just take a shot in the dark. He was calculating, and he was relying on Johnson, but he also had other influence in Washington.

The Boeing Air Transport Company

In January 1927, Boeing won the coveted mail route. The bid was a shock to everyone. Hubbard's figures said they could haul the mail halfway across the United States for $1.50 a pound for the first 1,000 miles and $.15 a pound for each additional 100 miles. Western Air Express's president, Harris Hanshue (Fig. 3-11), filed a bitter protest in Washington. He fully expected to win the bid and had made plans to expand. He had been carrying the mail from Los Angeles to Salt Lake City, for $3.00 a pound and bid $4.47 a pound for the new route.[15]

Others joined Hanshue's protest. No one could believe what Boeing had done. The others were bidding for profits, not a manufacturing outlet. It was impossible, they said, for anyone to carry the mail 1,950 miles at those rates. Boeing would ruin the private-contract system and could not operate safely under such rates. The protesters stated further that Boeing's factory would bear the real costs, and that was un-American. Boeing saw it as just the opposite: American free enterprise at work.

Boeing ignored the protests. He was gambling on an untried Wasp engine in a plane the U.S. Post Office had ignored. The other bidders almost

---

15. Kenn C. Rust, "Early Airlines," Part II, *American Aviation Historical Society Journal* (Winter 1985): 371.

3-11 Western Air Express's Harris Hanshue.

Smithsonian Institution

convinced the Post Office that Boeing's bid was not reliable. The Post Office required Boeing to post a $500,000 bond to insure performance of the contract. Boeing put up the money from his own funds.

Once the bond was in the hands of the Post Office, they changed their tune. They said, "The financial responsibility of this company is regarded by the Postmaster General as beyond question, while the practical part of the business is under the direction of Edward Hubbard, who has flown the oldest established contract operated under the Post Office ... ."

To fly the mail, Boeing formed a new company, the Boeing Air Transport Company (BAT). This company then contracted with the Boeing Airplane Company (BAC) to build 24 mailplanes. Phil Johnson became president of BAT, Eddie Hubbard became vice president of operations, and Clair Egtvedt became general manager. Boeing became chairman of BAT, ensuring that there would be harmony and a single business interest as a goal. The Boeing Company had in its original charter, "...to act as a common carrier of passengers and freight," and this was their opportunity. Boeing had built some 500 military planes and now he would see his dream come true: to serve the public.

3-12 Fred Rentschler at the time he was president of Pratt & Whitney.

When Johnson approached the Navy with Boeing's engine dilemma, he met resistance. Boeing did not want to upset the rapport between Johnson and the Navy, so he called in his big guns. His friend Fred Rentschler was president of the Pratt & Whitney Engine Company (Fig. 3-12).

Boeing also had a five-man lobby in Washington, whom he paid $86,000 a year—big money in those days—and he expected results. With Rentschler pressing the Navy from one side and the Washington lobby from the other, Boeing got what he wanted. Since there was no threat of war on the horizon, the Navy agreed to fall back 25 places in the Pratt & Whitney production schedule. This freed up the engines for Boeing's new mailplanes.

Boeing did come up with an idea whose evolution would tie in directly with the growth of commercial aviation and the Model 247. While the Wasp engines were still on the assembly line, Boeing suggested they modify the Model 40 by adding two seats in the small enclosed cabin between the wings.

3-13 The Boeing Model 80.

attendants. The flight stewardess, an innovation of a Boeing manager, sat on a jump seat in the rear of the cabin.

The initial success of the Model 80 led to improvements (Fig. 3-13). The Model 80, equipped with three 410-horsepower Wasps, was followed by twelve 15- to 18-passenger 80-As equipped with three 525-horsepower Pratt & Whitney Hornet engines. The twelfth 80-A was completed as the 80-B (Figs. 3-14 and 3-15) at the request of old-time pilots who were not quite sold on the enclosed pilot compartment. They felt they needed wind in their face to tell how the plane was flying. The pilots soon found merits in the new idea and the 80-B was converted to an 80-A.

Another feature Boeing advertised was that all the instruments were now on the panel in front of the pilots, not outside on the engines as was common in the Ford Tri-Motors. (see Fig. 3-16.)

The Boeing 80-A, described as "rocking chair" comfortable, was also one of the few aircraft that had a perfect passenger safety record. None of the twelve manufactured ever had a fatal accident, although several were written off after landing accidents. This would be of great publicity value when Boeing introduced the Model 247.

Following service modifications that changed fuel capacity, streamlined engine cowlings, and added more rudder areas, these twelve became 80-A1 models (Fig. 3-17). The eleventh 80-A was completed as a deluxe oil company executive transport under the designation Model 226 (Fig. 3-18).

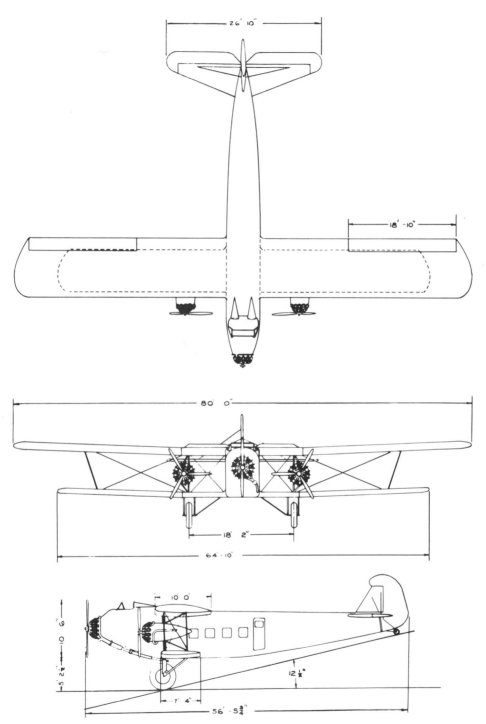

3-14 A three-view sketch of the Boeing Model 80-B.   Henry M. Holden Collection

3-15 The Boeing 80-B. Note the open cockpit.

3-16 A cockpit view of the port-engine oil pressure and temperature gauges, located outside on the engine spar.

    The first trimotor flights Boeing scheduled between Oakland, California, and Salt Lake City, Utah, flew at night—between 8:00 P.M. and 2:30 A.M.— and carried mail only. The 634-mile flights were in preparation of extending the San Francisco to Chicago leg of the route. On this route a pilot and copilot flew up to 18 passengers at a fare of $200 each, plus the mail, between the Golden Gate and the Great Lakes in 20 to 22½ hours. That was three

3-17 The Boeing Model 80A-1 in flight.

3-18 The Model 226. Note the casual copilot with an arm out the window.

times faster than the fastest extra-fare train in the country.[19] At Chicago, these flights connected with trimotors of Stout Airlines that continued on to Detroit and Cleveland.

19. Kenn C. Rust "Early Airlines," Chapter 5, *American Aviation Historical Society Journal* (Summer 1986): 114.

The Boeing 80-A flew for Boeing until the introduction of the Model 247. One 80-A went to the Boeing School of Aeronautics at Oakland, California, and another became an electrical signboard for night advertising in the Los Angeles area before being sent to Alaska during World War II. Today one sits quietly in the Boeing Museum of Flight in Seattle, Washington.

Transcontinental Air Transport (TAT) considered buying the $75,000 Model 80, but the $55,000 price tag of the Ford Tri-Motor was more attractive.[20] They never approached Boeing and no doubt if they had would probably have been turned away, as they were just a few short years later.

Boeing expansion

With the success of the BAT mailplanes still fresh in his mind, Boeing decided to expand his routes. His company had flown 815,256 miles with 298,372 pounds of mail and 525 passengers. The low bid was enough for BAT to earn a profit, just as Hubbard had predicted.

The 40-A and the Wasp engine were a good combination. In 8,282 hours there were only five minor instances of mechanical failure on the Wasp engines, and they averaged 300 hours between overhauls.[21] The planes logged 2,300 flights and only ten aircraft suffered minor damage—remarkable when you consider the terrain and conditions facing the transcontinental mail pilot in those days.[22]

Boeing's success in flying the mail in the face of dismal failures all around him lay in the efficiency of the Wasp engine, he said later. For a full year, he was the only one using the air-cooled radial engine. The Wasp was lighter and he replaced the weight of the radiator and water with mail, which meant another $400 revenue per trip. Within two years Boeing Air Transport had flown 5.6 million miles—the first airline to do so on a regular schedule.

The longest (1,152 miles) and most lucrative route on the West Coast was between Los Angeles, and Seattle. It was, however, already spoken for by Vern Gorst and his Pacific Air Transport (PAT).

Gorst ran his airline on a shoestring and often could not meet his payroll. He kept his pilots working by paying them in stock when cash was scarce. Several of his planes had crashed and Gorst decided he needed new planes if he was to stay in business. The old ones were costing him too much to maintain and repair.

---

20. R.E.G. Davies, *Airliners of the United States Since 1914*. (Washington, D.C.: Smithsonian Institution Press, 1982), 60.
21. Kenn C. Rust, "Early Airlines" Part II, *American Aviation Historical Society Journal* (Winter 1985): 277.
22. Ibid.

Gorst had four 40-B mailplanes[23] and went to Boeing to buy more, but $25,000 was a stiff price for a plane in those days. Gorst just could not afford it, nor could he get the financing. In addition, good old American competition had reared its head in the form of Western Air Express and Maddux Airlines.

W.A. Patterson—Office boy to company president

Western Air Express offered to buy out Gorst's stock at $250 a share. Gorst refused because there were no provisions for the employees or the stockholders. Boeing stepped in and offered Gorst $200 a share and a guarantee that he would keep all the employees on the payroll. After all, Boeing would need them to work the route he was trying to buy. In early 1928, Gorst accepted Boeing's offer. Shortly after the deal, Boeing brought in the man behind the scenes, W.A. (Pat) Patterson (Fig. 3-19), a young loan officer at Wells Fargo Bank in San Francisco.

W.A. Patterson went on to become a central figure in the nation's air transport industry for four decades. He served as United Airlines' president for 29 years before his election as chairman of the board in 1963. He retired from the board in 1966 but remained active as a consultant for the company.[24]

Patterson started as an office boy and advanced to assistant to the vice president in charge of new accounts at Wells Fargo Bank in San Francisco. In that position Patterson had recommended a small loan to Gorst at Pacific Air Transport.

Patterson came to the attention of Phil Johnson, and Johnson offered him a post as his assistant in Seattle in 1929. Patterson accepted and one of his first jobs was to round up every share of Gorst's old stock. He did, and the sudden demand for the once nearly worthless stock caused it to jump to over $600 per share.

The Johnson-Patterson combination worked perfectly. Johnson—who was cool, succinct, methodical, and hard-nosed—meshed perfectly with the warm, outgoing, quick, and imaginative Patterson. Until Patterson was 27, he had nothing to do with airplanes. His only travel was from his birthplace, Hawaii, to San Francisco at the age of 13 in a very slow boat. Suddenly he was in the middle of the industry.

As United Airlines general manager, he moved to Chicago in 1931 to establish the company's headquarters. In 1933 Patterson became a vice pres-

---

23. R.E.G. Davies, *Airliners of the United States Since 1914.* (Washington, D.C.: Smithsonian Institution Press, 1982), 70.

24. W.A. Patterson biographical files, Boeing Company.

3-19 W.A. Patterson.

The Boeing Company Archives

ident of United Airlines, and in April of the following year, at the age of 34, he was elected president. His "Rule of Five" (safety, passenger comfort, dependability, honesty, and sincerity) would be a major factor in his success and in molding the character of United Airlines.

United Aircraft and Transport— An unbeatable combination

Most people recognized Boeing as a superb administrator, but Boeing himself was not the main idea man in his company. He surrounded himself with idea men, top designers, and engineers. Hubbard was an idea man, and Egtvedt and Johnson were the engineers who built on Hubbard's ideas.

Boeing suffered a major but temporary setback when he lost Eddie Hubbard. Hubbard was in Salt Lake City when he suddenly became ill. He was rushed to the hospital, and after emergency surgery Hubbard decided to write his last will and testament. For a man who had spent a lifetime risking his life, he suddenly realized his human frailties. This even-tempered man who ate rain-soaked sandwiches in a cockpit to save time on mail flights died in December 1928 at the age of 39. He left an estate of more than $1 million.[25] One reason his estate was so big was his philosophy. He always set aside one-third of his income for gas and oil, one-third for maintenance, and one-third for "depreciation"—a euphemism for a crash, something he rarely had.

In 1928, American business was booming. Expansion was a measure of success and Boeing was prospering. At a staff meeting in late 1928, an idea bubbled to the surface. The Boeing Aircraft Company and Fred Rentschler's Pratt & Whitney Engine Company were doing remarkably well collaborating on military and commercial planes. Why not make the cooperation official with a merger? All the conditions were right. Charles Lindbergh's accomplishments had made aviation, although not popular with the masses, a household word. Aviation stocks were flying high on Wall Street, and mergers were popular ways of consolidating power.

Fred Rentschler started out as a puddler making cast-iron fittings for steam engines. His attention shifted to gasoline engines and by World War I he was the government's representative at the Wright-Martin Company. After the war he formed the Wright Aeronautical Company and helped lay the groundwork for the Whirlwind engine.

In the spring of 1925, the Navy wanted a dependable radial engine of 400-horsepower that weighed less than the government standard Liberty engine. Together with George Mead, he formed the Pratt & Whitney Engine Company. They bought a vacant tobacco factory and by December 1925, the Wasp engine was up and running.[26] This air-cooled engine quickly showed the shortcomings of the bulky plumbing in the liquid-cooled engines. The Wasp engine would help Pratt & Whitney grow and eventually supply 85 percent of the horsepower used by U.S. forces in World War II.[27]

A few weeks later the merger idea became a reality. The Boeing Aircraft and Transport Company, a holding company, controlled the stock of the Boeing Airplane Company and Boeing Aircraft and Transport. The stock went public and it sold quickly.

On February 1, 1929, Boeing took the next step and formed one of the largest aviation holding companies in the world, called United Aircraft & Transport Company (UAT), with its headquarters in Hartford, Connecticut. Fred Rentschler, president of Pratt & Whitney, swapped 800,000 shares of stock in his company for the new company's stock. Bill Boeing did the same,

---

25. Hubbard biographical files, NASM.
26. Rentschler biographical files, NASM.
27. Ibid.

turning over all his stock for the new United stock. Boeing became chairman and Rentschler president of the new combine.

Next Boeing entered into an agreement with the Huffar-Breaching Shipyard of Vancouver, Canada, a large yacht-building company. Boeing formed the Boeing Aircraft Company of Canada, Ltd. to manufacture Seattle-designed airplanes in Canada. The combine then bought Chance Vought, a manufacturer of Navy fighter planes, and the Hamilton Propeller Company (later Hamilton-Standard). The Hamilton Metalplane Company of Milwaukee also joined the gaggle and continued to manufacture airplanes of its own design.

The success of these mergers prompted Boeing to see even greater potential on the aviation scene. Rentschler and Boeing immediately began collecting strays, much like in the Monopoly board game. They rounded up Sikorsky Aviation Company, a New England manufacturer of amphibious craft, and Stearman Aircraft Company of Wichita, Kansas. Standard Steel Propeller and Stout Airlines were next into the fold. The seeds of today's United Airlines system were beginning to sprout, and UAT had more than $146 million in capital assets.[28]

National Air Transport also played an important role in Boeing's plans. NAT had won the New York to Chicago route with a bid of $1.24 a pound. With that route, Boeing would own a coast-to-coast route.

On March 30, 1930, UAT bought one-third interest in NAT. When Clement Keys, head of North American Aviation, found out, he immediately took steps to head off a takeover of NAT. At the April 17 shareholders' meeting, Keys attempted to implement some bylaws to block the proxy votes that Rentschler was about to make representing the UAT interests. While the proxy battle raged, Rentschler quietly gathered additional proxy votes. Keys's motion was ruled illegal and when the vote was taken he discovered that Rentschler commanded 57 percent of the NAT votes.

In a subsequent meeting on April 23, Rentschler went looking to make peace. Keys was absent from this meeting, a clear sign that the UAT forces had won.[29] Soon after, UAT bought the remaining NAT stock, and National Air Transport came into the fold with routes from Dallas to New York City and Chicago. On August 30, United transferred Stout Airlines into National Air Transport, and NAT began passenger and mail service between New

---

28. R.E.G. Davies, *Airliners of the United States Since 1914*. (Washington, D.C.: Smithsonian Institution Press, 1982), 71.
29. Ibid, 75.

York and Chicago, giving UAT the first coast-to-coast passenger and mail route.

Rentschler and Boeing were on a roll. UAT was quickly becoming the largest airline conglomerate in the United States. BAT was the first to fly passengers at night, on scheduled flights, and over long distances. Now was not the time to become complacent.

Varney Airlines, run by a World War I pilot, Walter T. Varney, consisted of a flying school, an air ferry service, and an airmail service between Pasco, Washington, and Elko, Nevada. When bidding opened, Varney figured no one would want the route and he was right. His $1.25 a pound was the only bid.

He started with six Swallow biplanes equipped with 160-horsepower Curtiss engines. From there he picked up faster planes and began to branch out. His expansion was going so well, he needed more and faster planes. He went to Boeing to order nine 40B-4 planes, which held four passengers and used the powerful Pratt & Whitney, nine-cylinder Hornet engine. However, like many airline companies that expanded too fast, he ran out of money and could not afford the capital investment.

Boeing saw a good deal waiting in the routes that Varney held, and he made an offer. Varney accepted and United Aircraft & Transport began to look like a big airline company. As of June 30, 1930, UAT had routes north to Seattle, and northwest from Salt Lake City to Seattle.

An interlocking directorate

This gathering of stray birds resulted in so much activity that United Aircraft & Transport formed a new operating company known as United Airlines (UAL). To maintain the growing positive image the airlines were building, the individual lines continued to function under their original names.[30]

Rentschler took a more active role in the Monopoly-style game than Boeing did and followed the time-proven J.P. Morgan style of consolidation. He exchanged stock in the new UAT company for ownership in the smaller company, and UAT continued to grow. By the time Boeing and Rentschler were finished consolidating smaller airlines, United Aircraft & Transport would have 120 planes in the air, covering more than 32,000 miles a day. This made them the largest aviation company in the country.[31] By the spring of 1931, UAT was being called the "world's largest air transport system."[32]

---

30. Peter Bowers, *Boeing Aircraft Since 1916* (New York: Funk and Wagnalls, 1968) 30.

31. Harold Mansfield, *Vision* (New York: Duell, Sloan, & Pearce, 1956), 102.

32. R.E.G. Davies, *Airliners of the United States Since 1914.* (Washington, D.C.: Smithsonian Institution Press, 1982), 79.

Both the airline and manufacturing sides grew stronger, and the consolidations had a marked effect on Boeing activity. Pratt & Whitney engines and Hamilton Standard propellers became standard on all Boeing planes unless the customer specified another arrangement. Each company retained its own identity by keeping its name and its product line. The presence of more than one airplane manufacturer in one corporation was compatible because their product lines were not competitive.

Rentschler and Boeing had set up an enormous interlocking directorate and both profited beyond anyone's comprehension. The mergers took place during the peak of the Wall Street boom. Rentschler bought his P&W stock at $.25 a share. The stock split 78 – 1 and he exchanged them for the new company's stock at 2.2 shares for each original share. (Someone who paid $40 for 200 shares of P&W would have found them increased to almost 35,000 shares of UAT.) Fred Rentschler's original investment of $316.25, for which he received 1,265 shares, grew to $35,578,848 by May 1929.[33]

Bill Boeing, already a millionaire, became richer. He had invested $480,000 in Boeing Aircraft and Transport. While the merger was in the works, he bought another 4,319 shares of BAT at $.06 a share. He exchanged them for United stock at the rate of 12 for 1. The stock zoomed upward, earning Boeing $5,332,284 from a $259 investment.[34]

The Boeing-Rentschler combine gobbled up more than 40 percent of the aviation business. The combine began looking like the early Robber Barons of Standard Oil and duPont. Any plane that rolled out of the Boeing, Sikorsky, or Vought plants had Rentschler's Pratt & Whitney engines equipped with Hamilton Standard propellers and Stearman landing gear—all products of United Aircraft & Transport.

McNary-Watres Act

During this period of mergers, transfers, and buyouts, there were significant developments and political hocus-pocus going on in Washington.

The Republican Postmaster General appointed under the Hoover administration had remained out of the airmail picture until, in a surprise move on February 19, 1930, Walter F. Brown appeared before a Congressional committee to recommend passage of the McNary-Watres Bill, an amendment to the 1925 Air Mail Act.

Brown was a lawyer from Toledo and knew nothing about aviation when he took the job, but he quietly studied the industry for a year. What he dis-

---

33. Carl Solberg, *Conquest of the Skies*, (Little Brown Co., 1979), 62.
34. Ibid.

covered was an industry near chaos. The country was criss-crossed with a jigsaw of little airlines. Small, poorly financed airlines were fighting big ones. Others were flying the same routes, trying to undercut the larger companies. Many airlines existed only because of the airmail they flew, making little effort to lure passengers. The industry was haphazard and unstable, and dangerous conditions resulted.

Brown knew he had to bring order to the chaos among the 36 scheduled airlines and 7 foreign lines flying in the United States. Of the 36, 17 flew mail on 25 routes. Between 1928 and 1929 at least 32 airlines came into existence in the United States, although some failed soon after their first flight.[35]

The McNary-Watres Bill was the tool Brown needed, and it gave him power to do something about the problem. He saw the future of the airlines not in carrying mail only, but in flying mail and people within the framework of a regulated network of airlines.

Some people have accused Brown of favoritism, backroom politics, and dictatorship. His proponents called him fair, perceptive, and an enlightened savior. It is to his credit that he was responsible for creating the major air carriers we have today.

Brown wanted three strongly financed, competitive, transcontinental routes and two coastal routes, each run by a separate company feeding the smaller airlines. With five major air carriers serving America, he saw the multiple overhead, the inefficiencies of frequent changes of ownership, and the use of many types of equipment over the same airway (like Universal Air Lines System operating three mail routes using two different types of aircraft and operating five types of planes on its passenger routes) giving way to efficiency and economies not possible under the existing system (Figs. 3-20 through Fig. 3-23).[36]

Brown was instrumental in having the terms of the mail contracts tailored to fit the airlines he felt were the most profitable. In order to build efficiency into the system, he forced some airlines that were on the verge of bankruptcy to merge. One merger between two reluctant airlines turned out to be one of the most successful in history.

There had been strong words of a monopoly with the formation of the United Aircraft and Transport combine, and Brown wanted to head off a political target for the Democrats. Transcontinental Air Transport had never flown an airmail route of more than 250 miles at night, and Western Air Express had extended themselves thin with routes blanketing the southwest.[37]

---

35. Kenn C. Rust, "Early Airlines," Chapter 3, *American Aviation Historical Society Journal* (Spring 1986): 62.

36. Ibid, 63.

37. Frank Taylor, *High Horizons* (New York: McGraw-Hill, 1962), 78.

American Airlines

3-20 The American Airplane and Engine Company built this metal-canvas-wood passenger plane in 1931. Twenty-one of these 575-horsepower single-engine planes were built, and American Airways withdrew them just three years later.

TWA

3-21 The 18-passenger Curtiss Condor transport was an early transport of the Transcontinental Air Transport Company, later known as TWA.

The birth of United Aircraft & Transport 1925 – 1930 **65**

3-22 This Stinson Model "T" trimotor appeared in 1930. Made of wood and canvas, it reputedly gained 50 pounds payload by using a color scheme with the lightest pigments available: black and gold. This trimotor carried 10 passengers. Note that the wing braces on the Stinson were absent on the Ford Tri-Motor.

3-23 American Airlines used converted bombers as passenger planes. This airplane still had the military paint scheme on the tail.

Transcontinental Air Transport had been incorporated on May 16, 1928, and capitalized at $5 million. With Charles Lindbergh as the main mover, it was doing well. TAT had bought up the Maddux Airline with its Ford Tri-Motors and had helped the line make money. On June 30, 1930, Postmaster Brown forced a very reluctant Harris Hanshue of the financially strapped Western

Air Express to partially merge with TAT-Maddux, forming Transcontinental and Western Air (T&WA). Western Airlines had to sell its Los Angeles to Dallas route to American Airways and its Kansas City line to the new T&WA. These routes were both duplicated by the other two airlines.

This route duplication among many of the airlines provided Brown with a common but odd background to force mergers. It was Brown's way of helping spur along the coast-to-coast airway system he had in mind.

By the end of the year, Western had cut its payroll from 410 to 133 people and was forced to sell many of its planes. It had, however, managed to stay solvent and by the end of the year had ended its relationship with T&WA. The T&WA merger now formed the second transcontinental airline, from New York to Los Angeles, and eliminated the specter of a monopoly by United Aircraft and Transport.[38]

UAT—The winning combination

The largest airline expansions had been on those carrying mail and passengers. The majority of those lines had carried both on the same planes. However, as airmail loads increased, the schedules of departures and arrivals at such inconvenient hours resulted in a growing tendency to separate mail and passengers. Brown looked at the Boeing combine and saw the pattern he wanted for the industry. Boeing was one of the few airmail contractors who had invested heavily in new planes and adequate accommodations for passengers. Boeing continued to fly mail and passengers and was using the luxurious Model 80-A (Figs. 3-24 and 3-25). Many airlines had switched to smaller planes that were less expensive to operate, and some had stopped flying passengers altogether.

National Air Transport, before being bought by UAT, had also switched to all-mail in their five Ford Tri-Motors between New York, Chicago, and Dallas. This switch was not subtle, either. They raised the passenger fare from $100 to $200. Then they gave each passenger a flying suit and parachute, and more often than not the passenger sat with a sack of mail in his lap. NAT flew only 168 passengers that way.[39] The mail was cheaper to fly than people, easier to handle, and didn't complain (Fig. 3-26).

This situation should not be blamed on NAT alone. The U.S. Post Office did precipitate the conditions. In 1928, they reduced the airmail rate from $.06 to $.05. This caused a phenomenal increase in the use of airmail. NAT had an 83 percent increase in its business. In the first four weeks of August, it

---

38. "Beating the Odds, The First Sixty Years of Western Airlines," (no author) 9.
39. R.E.G. Davies, *Airliners of the United States Since 1914*. (Washington, D.C.: Smithsonian Institution Press, 1982), 46.

3-24 The Boeing 80-A shown here loading mail and Express.

3-25 William Boeing (left) next to a Model 80A.

carried 113,461 pounds, compared to 62,098 pounds the month before, and it flew 224 schedules in 28 days.[40]

It was evident to Brown that, without some incentive, the carriers would not push for improvements in passenger service, which for the most part was only a small portion of their revenues.

On April 29, 1930, the McNary-Watres Bill became law, and Brown had the muscle he needed to accomplish his mission. There were three provisions behind the bill that gave him clout.

---

40. *NAT Bulletin Board* #9 (September 14, 1928).

3-26 A National Air Transport Ford Tri-Motor.

First, it established a space-per-mile rate for carrying mail, instead of the previous pound-per-mile rate. The government said it would pay for predetermined space whether it was filled with mail or not. The impact of this provision was significant since the rate was only $1.25 per mile.[41] To further encourage passenger service, the rate would be reduced over a five-year period to make the lines self-sustaining. There would be extra pay for such extras as night flying, passenger seats, flying over mountains, and other so-called "variables"[42] to encourage operators to buy larger planes to carry people.

The award of a contract would be to the lowest responsible bidder who had operated scheduled service over a 250-mile route for six months. This automatically eliminated the fly-by-day operators. United Aircraft and Transport had already proven its reliability in Brown's eyes.

The second provision guaranteed to successful operators continued success. Any line operating for two years could trade in mail route contracts for a route certification good for ten years, revokable only for "willful neglect." UAT had also fulfilled this provision.

The third and most powerful provision gave Brown almost godlike power to wheel and deal when needed to extend or consolidate routes "when in

41. Kenn C. Rust "Early Airlines," Chapter 5, *American Aviation Historical Society Journal* (Summer 1986): 111.

42. Frank Taylor, *High Horizons* (New York: McGraw-Hill, 1962), 74.

his judgment the public interest would be promoted." Brown used this power so effectively that the president of the United States would eventually have to step in.

Brown's power was a double-edged sword for Boeing. It spelled doom for one Boeing venture but set the stage for another.

Right after the passage of the McNary-Watres Act, Postmaster Brown called a meeting in Washington of the major airline executives. The meeting was to discuss the "distribution of the new (transcontinental) airmail contracts," and would later have far-reaching and dire consequences for the industry. In meetings that lasted into late June, the parties agreed unanimously that the Postmaster General should act as umpire in "settling and working out such arrangements that might be necessary to establish the transcontinental lines."[43] Air transport got its start in airmail and now it was time, Brown felt, to push it into the passenger business.

Merger fever

During this period, Boeing was not the only one buying up small airlines. There was merger fever. American Airways bought up several smaller southwest airlines, including a small airline that flew single-engine monoplanes between Atlanta and Dallas/Fort Worth. With Delta Air Service in the fold, American Airways had the southeast link and formed the third coast-to-coast route.

The three routes Brown planned were now in place. Tony Fokker's American company lost its identity when General Motors formed a conglomerate during the aero-merger boom of 1929. By the time the merger fever had passed in 1931, no less than 18 airlines had ceased to be separate operators.[44]

The financial picture grew brighter for Boeing, thanks to the good postmaster some called Boss Brown. When the time came for the airlines to put on bigger planes as the McNary Act had intended, United Aircraft worked out a nifty arrangement. Boeing would make the new planes, with Pratt & Whitney supplying the engines and Hamilton Standard the propellers, and the orders placed by the subsidiary airlines BAT, NAT, PAT, and Varney would be large enough to ensure a profit to all, but keep the factory so busy it could not sell outside the combine—at least not for a few years.

This plan would result in a fatal logistical error. For the present, however, Rentschler and Boeing had achieved the goal they had aimed for back in 1927.

---

43. Ibid, 115.
44. Kenn C. Rust, "Early Airlines," Chapter 7, *American Aviation Historical Society Journal* (Fall 1986): 162.

4

The Monomail
1930–1932

The world was growing 'smaller because of aviation, and a new philosophy was evolving in aircraft design and manufacturing techniques. The biplane and trimotor (Fig. 4-1) were slowly giving way to the monoplane and twin-engine, while the tubular-frame, fabric-covered fuselage would also give way to the monocoque fuselage, the cantilever wing, and an all-metal skin.

Otto Junkers had been designing all-metal planes in Europe since World War I, but the idea and technology had not caught on in America (Figs. 4-2 and 4-3). In the early 1920s, a few American designers tried metal, but no one stayed with the design. The metals were too heavy and there were no engines powerful enough to lift the weight. It was not until aluminum alloys like duralumin came along that metal construction got a serious second look.

The idea of all-metal airplanes had evolved slowly in the United States. Most airplane manufacturers used some metal in the fabric-covered mail and passenger planes. The Boeing mailplanes used metal walls in the mail compartment so the mailbag locks did not tear the fabric skin, and metal plates allowed accessibility to the engine controls. Ford's and Junker's trimotors and Britain's first all-metal, trimotored, low-wing cantilever monoplane, the Beardmore-Rockland-Flexall, were the exceptions.

Eddie Hubbard and Clair Egtvedt were brainstorming one day when the idea for an all-metal airplane for Boeing's company came to them. As Hubbard put it, "We just started with the idea of extending the metal from nose to tail."

The two were sharing a hotel room during a business trip when Hubbard started thinking aloud. Egtvedt grabbed a piece of the hotel's stationery and

4-1 The Ford Tri-Motor shown here undergoing maintenance and inspection by the curious.

4-2 A Junkers JU-52 trimotor. Note the uncowled nose engine on this museum piece.

4-3 This Junkers JU-52 until recently was still flying in the United States in the air show circuit. It was called "Iron Annie" by its owner-writer, Martin Cadin.

started sketching what they discussed. First he drew a long, slender wing. Egtvedt was moderately enthusiastic about the idea, although it went against the conservative Boeing philosophy. "The easiest way to work with metal," he said, "is to use round shapes."

Hubbard watched as Egtvedt drew a round circle on the wing. "Here's your metal plane, Eddie, and it has practically no drag. Not like those flying washboards." Egtvedt was, of course, referring to the corrugated metal skin of the Fords and Junkers.

Egtvedt's diagram was an oversimplification, but it got their creative juices going.

"When you put wheels on it, you introduce drag," said Egtvedt.

"Suppose we pull the wheels up into the body of the plane? That would solve your drag problem."

Egtvedt raised his eyebrows. It sounded good.

Then the practical side of Hubbard surfaced. "Yes, but can we do it? Let's say we can," he said, "then how much will it cost?"

"There are many roadblocks," said Egtvedt. "A smooth metal skin would need more internal support. We'd have to use thicker metal or more support inside." Egtvedt thought for a moment and then said, "Perhaps we should give this monocoque construction another look? It will cost money and no one has any real experience with it."

Historical perspective—European ideas

In the early years of aviation, Germany and France led the world in aviation research and development. European aircraft designers recognized that, although struts made the plane stronger, they also introduced drag and cut back significantly on the aircraft's efficiency.

The French began experimenting with a method of construction called *monocoque* (pronounced "mono-cock," and French for "single shell"). They lined the fuselage walls with glued sheets of plywood. In theory, the walls would carry the entire load under the flight dynamics. In practice, however, they found the planes still needed inner support, especially the wings. They had the right idea, but the materials were heavy, often too heavy to allow the plane to take off or to maintain stable flight.

Germany had published studies on the greater efficiency resulting from streamlined aircraft. Hugo Junkers, a German aeronautical scientist, designed the cantilever wing with metal spars covered with corrugated metal; it was an efficient wing that needed no external bracing. In 1919, Junkers first used this construction with an all-metal, aluminum alloy called *duralumin* in a low-wing airliner, the F-13, dubbed the "steel duck." Duralumin was lighter than aluminum but twice as strong.

Another German, Dr. Adolf Rohrbach, adapted Junker's all-metal technique and calculated that, by reducing skin friction, airflow efficiency would be improved. In 1919, he worked out a significant compromise. He discovered that a lightweight, smooth metal skin could bear a good deal of the load if the skin had a boxlike arrangement of metal spars for interior reinforcement. It was a semi-monocoque type of construction and a significant step toward eliminating the wires and braces in aircraft design.

Rohrbach continued to experiment with duralumin. He carefully positioned two pieces of this metal and welded them together, thereby increasing the strength of the metal. He called it *stressed skin* and applied this veneered metal to a series of planes he built around 1923. Although his airplanes were not successful for other reasons, the stressed-skin principle was sound.

Anthony Fokker, a Dutch designer influenced by Rohrbach and Junkers, began using cantilever wing structures covered with wood and fabric. Junker's all-metal planes and Fokker's plywood and fabric-covered aircraft were successful and popular among the airlines in the 1920s.

Metal designs in America

American William Stout, borrowing from the European pioneers, began experimenting with these new ideas. He built an all-metal airplane for the U.S. Army, but it crashed and the Army lost interest. He applied the same principles to a monoplane transport he called the "Air Sedan." Henry Ford bought Stout's design and it grew into the famous Ford Tri-Motor.

By 1926, Rohrbach had refined his technique using newly developed aluminum alloys. In a lecture the following year before the Society of Automotive Engineers in Los Angeles, Rohrbach discussed the possibilities of putting all the airplane's load on a smooth "stressed skin."

At the time, the only all-metal passenger planes were the German Junkers and their American counterpart, the Ford Tri-Motor, both of which had corrugated skins running span-wise that created additional aerodynamic problems. The drag in the grooves was much worse than first believed. Although the corrugations stiffened the skin in one direction, they rendered the skin unsuitable for bearing loads perpendicular to the corrugations.[1]

Jack Northrop, a young designer attending Rohrbach's lecture, began to think through Rohrbach's revolutionary idea. Northrop had begun his career alongside Arthur Raymond in Donald Douglas's drafting room, and was among America's promising young aircraft designers.

At home one evening, Northrop began to sketch the outline of a monocoque fuselage with little external bracing and wire. "It was a radical design in those days, far removed from the more conventional types Douglas was building," he said, "but I felt he would be interested."[2] Northrop also wanted a share in the company that built his design, but with Douglas this was not possible.

When Northrop couldn't talk Douglas into building the design, he moved on to Lockheed. He refined Rohrbach's original idea, and when his design rolled out of the shop in 1927 he called it the *Vega*. The high-wing monoplane had 35 percent more cabin space, was lighter, and had less aerodynamic drag than if it had used the old-style construction. Wiley Post flew it around the world in less than nine days in 1931 and established a solid reputation for Lockheed and Northrop.

The *Vega* was made from wood and the original model, introduced in 1927, did not have an engine cowling to smooth the blunt contours of the radial engine or wheel covers to streamline the fixed landing gear. The streamlined fuselage of molded plywood, topped by a cantilever wing, incorporated Rohrbach's technique of stressed skin only in plywood construction. After an engine cowling and wheel covers were added, the plane's top speed increased from 135 to 155 miles per hour—a convincing argument for more research into aerodynamic streamlining.

Northrop left Lockheed and formed his own company to build the first metal plane of semi-monocoque construction. The Northrop Alpha (Fig. 4-4)

---

1. Frank Howard and Bill Gunston, *Conquest of the Air* (New York: Random House, 1972) 169.

2. George Vecsey, *Getting Off the Ground* (New York: E.P. Hutton, 1979), 235.

4-4 Northrop's Alpha.

had a metal skin backed by ¼-inch duralumin "stiffeners" that lined the interior like barrel hoops.

As innovative as this technique was, the wing was the real eye-opener. Northrop used a lightweight aluminum lattice of spars inside the wing. The smooth stressed-skin wing carried the entire weight of the plane. The underside of the wing carried the tension, and the upper side, the compression. The pilot could see the skin on the wings wrinkling between the ribs under the compression loads. Northrop also fitted the wing with fillets where it joined the fuselage. This feature enhanced its aerodynamic efficiency even more.

After seeing the Alpha, everyone began to take all-metal monoplane construction seriously. TWA used the Northrop Alpha type as part of its fleet of fast mailplanes. Although William Boeing's tubular metal airframe innovations and Rohrbach's stressed skin provided intellectual stimuli to men like Northrop, the idea of all-metal planes was still not a popular design.

After seeing Northrop's first creation, Clair Egtvedt knew stressed skin was the way future aerodynamically efficient planes would be built. He stated a reflection of Northrop's design technique: To make an airplane efficient, it should be shaped like a bullet without wires and struts. But this was easier said than done.

The conservative Boeing approach

If Eddie Hubbard was the inventive thinker and Egtvedt the believer in Hubbard's ideas, then Charles Monteith was the cautious counterbalance. When

Hubbard and Egtvedt took the idea of an all-metal plane to Monteith, he said no.

"You'll make it too heavy, and if you use thin metal it won't be strong enough."

Monteith did not like monoplane designs anyway. He thought they were unsafe. He had watched a friend fall to his death when the center section of an experimental monoplane fell away. He had seen another monoplane design develop flutter that tore off the wings, forcing the pilot to bail out. *Flutter* was a term for a vibration that might start in a wing and get worse until the plane came apart in flight.

"There are too many unknowns. We don't know how to control flutter, and we have no data on the cantilever design at high speeds (about 150 mph)," said Monteith.

Monteith didn't want to sound negative; he was stating the facts. He was part of the Boeing team and wanted to make the company a winner as much as the next person. He was also a realist, though. It was his job on the line if the idea didn't work.

Monteith was one of the best engineers in the country and was known to temper a situation with reason. He had written a textbook on aerodynamics that West Point and other universities were using. He had also been in charge of dozens of experimental designs while in the Army. A device like a retractable landing gear was a complicated mechanism and could cause mechanical problems. "Keep it simple and it's less likely things will go wrong," he said.

Monteith also saw the positive side of the argument. Sooner or later metal airplanes were going to be a fact of life. Slowly he yielded to Egtvedt, but with concessions.

In the beginning Hubbard was in favor of a metal plane on the size of the Model 80-A, which held eighteen passengers. He yielded on that point when Monteith reminded him of what he had said. "In bad weather we have to leave the Eighty in the barn and roll out the Forty-Bs." Monteith also reminded him he had once said, "I'd like smaller and faster planes and more of them. It gives us more flexibility. Speed is the showcase of air transportation. The Eighty is a lot of plane to handle, like flying a barn door in a Kansas windstorm."

Consensus engineering

Monteith also got Hubbard to agree to a small high-wing monoplane with external supports. Egtvedt yielded under the arguments but didn't like the idea. With that last concession they went to Boeing, who authorized design work on the high-wing monoplane. To keep all idea avenues open, Boeing decided to also authorize preliminary design work on the low-wing proposal. Egtvedt knew that, this way, the low-wing design would get a fair assessment.

As the design work went forward, it became obvious to the engineers that the low-wing version offered smoother lines. The high-wing design continued to evolve, yet the shape of the low-wing persisted. Some Boeing engineers would not let go of the possibilities. The engineer in Monteith began to feel it was right. He asked Boeing to allow the design work to continue. "Eddie may have something in that idea," he said.

Boeing agreed and encouraged them to continue. "We must not dismiss any new idea with the snap judgment that it cannot be done," Boeing said. "We are pioneering a new science, and we must explore every new avenue and idea. Any idea that may be an improvement must be investigated. We have proven that science and hard work can beat what appear to be impossible demands."[3]

Monteith, of course, agreed with Boeing, but he still had some doubts. The Boeing philosophy was practical, but expensive.

When the low-wing design began to look like it had real possibilities, Boeing authorized work on the prototype. From paper, it began to take shape in the factory. The monocoque construction looked like it would work, but the engineers still had questions that only physical tests would answer. With the aid of some Army research on wing bracing, Boeing engineers worked out a bridgelike structure inside the wing, thus eliminating all wires and struts on the outside.

Birth of the XB-9 bomber

While development of the low-wing design, now called the Monomail, was underway, Boeing was working on other warplane designs. International communications still left a lot to be desired. Boeing knew the Europeans were not sitting still in aviation development so he sent Egtvedt to Europe to investigate their progress.

Egtvedt toured the airplane plants in Europe and was not too impressed with what he saw. Europe had the same problem as the United States: a profusion of designs with little standardization. Claude Dornier's Do-X was one model that impressed him. The Do-X, Germany's twelve-engine biplane behemoth, carried 169 passengers. It particularly impressed Egtvedt because it carried enough fuel to cross the Atlantic. The structure, he noted, was simple but the engine arrangement was a mechanical nightmare. There were

---

3. Reynolds Phillips, "William Boeing," *Boeing Magazine* (November 1956).

twelve engines mounted on struts above the wings. A complex system of mechanical devices was needed to operate and synchronize the engines, and the devices were prone to mechanical failure.

None of the designs Egtvedt saw rivaled the simplicity of the monoplane under construction in Seattle. Egtvedt imagined someday there would be engines powerful enough to fly the Do-X's 169 passengers, and it would not require twelve of them. He did not think this would be for awhile, possibly decades. He was happy to stick to something small and simple.

In England, Egtvedt noticed new developments in British aeronautical technology. New British bombers had long, slender bodies, similar to the Monomail shape. Egtvedt began to wonder about a bomber design fashioned like the Monomail.

Bombers in those days, however, had a major restriction in their design. Most were biplanes or triplanes because they were the heavy weightlifters in military aviation. In aeronautical engineering, it was axiomatic that to carry the weight of bombs the plane needed a large wing area. The more wing area at a given speed, the more weight it could lift. Too large a wing, and the structural weight became prohibitive.

When Egtvedt returned to the United States, he talked about what he had seen in Europe. Almost casually he mentioned the idea of a monoplane bomber. Monteith, aware of the principle of the modern-day bomber, knew Egtvedt's idea didn't sound right. He did, however, speculate that with two or three powerful engines it probably would work.

Monteith was willing to study a monoplane design but suggested they get started on a metal biplane design. Everyone agreed. That was the safe, conservative road to travel. Two of the Army's mainline bombers were the Keystone and the Curtiss, both biplane designs. However, with Boeing's nod, Egtvedt and Johnson approached the Army with the monoplane idea.

The Army was cautiously receptive if Boeing could make the plane fast. None of the Army's bombers were very fast—most did around 100 miles per hour, which was too slow in daylight against faster pursuit planes and also too slow for outrunning the searchlights at night.

"How would you like to develop your bomber on speculation?" the Army replied. "We'd like to see what you are talking about."

When the two returned to Seattle, they discussed the Army's proposal with Boeing and Monteith. Boeing kept an open mind during the discussion. Johnson was in favor of developing a twin-engine monoplane prototype on speculation. Monteith was characteristically cautious. "Let's not bet on the wrong horse," he said. "We shouldn't move on a monoplane design until we've completely written off a biplane design."

Johnson countered, "Let's design it both ways. Then we can find out which one is better." Boeing like that idea.

The designs started out on equal footing: both monoplane and biplane would be designed around 600-horsepower engines. It soon became obvious which design was gaining. The reduction in drag presented by the smooth-metal monoplane design offset the lack of wing area. There was also an advantage in the cantilever wing of the monoplane. It gave more speed that was critical over an enemy target, although the wing area on the biplane translated into more payload.

The first concessions to the monoplane design were evident. Monteith's major concern remained in the questionable strength of the monoplane and the inherent wing flutter. To compound his anxiety, the Monomail had not yet flown and the bomber design was bigger, faster, and heavier.

Egtvedt and Johnson were still cautiously optimistic that the monoplane bomber design would work. So was the Army: they said it was the most progressive-looking bomber design they had ever seen. In January 1930, Washington gave Boeing the go-ahead, on speculation. Boeing would have to finance the project himself. Later he would find out why. Boeing's board approved the expenditure, confident that the design would win orders.

The Monomail

Built under the most secretive conditions, the commercial Monomail took the industry by complete surprise when it appeared on May 3, 1930. The plane was similar to the Alpha in its general layout but was a radical departure in design. The fuselage was almost round; the low wings were thick and tapered with an open cockpit above and behind each wing's trailing edge. The onlookers found the wings remarkable. They turned up and back slightly, and they made flying look natural (see Fig. 4-5).

The airplane's sleek appearance gave the impression that it could slice through the air like a bullet. It did not have struts, wires, or square edges like the Fords and Fokkers. The single nose-mounted 575-horsepower Pratt & Whitney Hornet engine, hidden inside a streamlined cowling, gave it a top speed of 158 miles per hour; and its tubelike forward section could hold half its gross weight. Even its color scheme was shocking: green fuselage, grey tail, orange wings. On the side of the fuselage was the name Monomail.

The public had never seen anything like the Monomail. Probably the most revolutionary feature other than the smooth metal skin and retractable landing gear was the adjustable-pitch propeller. This feature allowed the pilot to set the angle of the blades to get maximum aerodynamic efficiency at altitude. In theory it was supposed to be very effective on takeoff.

4-5 The wing bracing shown here on the XF7B-1 in 1933 was one of the secrets to Boeing's success with the low-wing cantilever design of the Monomail.

The design was far beyond the state of the art, and it resulted in intensive experimentation and the later development of the controllable-pitch propeller. Earlier mechanisms had operated mechanically and seemed to work only in smaller engines. The high stress placed on propellers by powerful engines had prevented further development of these early mechanical devices.

In the history of the Boeing Airplane Company, the development of the Monomail was the crucial turning point, comparable only to Boeing's decision in 1916 to build the plane that put him in the aircraft manufacturing business, the B&W. Paradoxically, the B&W was the only Boeing-built aircraft never given a model-number designation, and the Model 200, with the copyrighted name Monomail, was the first Boeing-built aircraft to be given a name and a model designation. The Monomail also would have another distinction: it would be the last single-engine commercial aircraft built by Boeing.

On May 3, 1930, the Monomail was ready for its maiden flight. The word whispered around Seattle now had a shape.

After a five minute warm-up, the Monomail was rolling down the runway gathering speed. At the last minute, Eddie Allen, the test pilot, aborted the take off (Fig. 4-6). Something was wrong.

Allen couldn't get enough lift. He struggled with the sleek, bullet-shaped

4-6 Eddie Allen.

fuselage but just couldn't get the plane into the air. The problem was easy to identify; the solution was not. The pitch of the propeller would give the plane great speed in the air, but acted like a fan blowing air away from the plane while it was on the ground.

By May 22, engineers had worked out a compromise setting, and Allen flew the plane through the initial tests with no additional problems. The problem that delayed the first flight still haunted them. They had altered the angle of the propeller so the plane could take off, but by doing so, robbed the plane of speed in the air. This was a serious problem at high-altitude airports, where the air was thinner and would seriously handicap the takeoff profile.

Hamilton Standard Propeller was part of the United Aircraft and Transport family, so Monteith turned to that company for an answer. What they gave him made him more anxious and uneasy. Frank Caldwell had just developed a controllable-pitch propeller, and he suggested they try it on the Monomail. The propeller would be set for one pitch on takeoff, and another, steeper angle once airborne.

The idea of a changeable-pitch propeller had been tried on war planes before World War I, but had never worked out. Although significant improvements in engine technology took place in Canada and England in the 1920s, it was Frank Caldwell who perfected the technique.

Monteith didn't like the idea. He said that kind of propeller would make the plane heavier, and it was another mechanical device that could break. He thought the answer was to increase the supercharging or air into the engine, thus increasing the power at altitude.[4]

After more tests, engineers arrived at another compromise: a smaller propeller without gears to shift its angle and increased propeller speed. With more propeller speed, the pitch was not as critical. Egtvedt agreed to the compromise but didn't feel it was the answer.

Gene Wilson, who was at the helm of Hamilton Standard, wanted a controllable-pitch device and a geared-down engine that would turn a larger propeller. These features, combined with enough supercharging, should give the plane more power at high altitude. His proposed solution was overkill and rejected by Monteith as too complicated.

McNary-Watres Act—
Another step toward chaos in the skies

On the other side of the country, events in Washington would doom the Monomail before it ever got off the ground. The McNary-Watres Bill had changed the rate structure for private operators carrying the U.S. mail. Boeing saw the political events like the McNary-Watres Act unfolding as his Monomail was taking shape, but he had missed a very important clue during the congressional battle to approve the bill. Boeing was left holding a fast mailplane that even when full could not break even.

The change the McNary-Watres Bill caused was so drastic that the Monomail, designed to carry mail only, was obsolete. Since the Monomail could not carry passengers, it couldn't reap the rewards of the new legislation, which paid a premium to airlines that carried passengers, not mail.

Boeing and Egtvedt began examining the facts. Should they scrap the Monomail? Egtvedt thought it could be modified to fly passengers instead of mail. Boeing thought so, too. Monteith was cautiously optimistic.

Boeing weighed the facts but one thing was obvious: without passengers, the Monomail was useless as a revenue-producing airplane. Boeing still felt he had a good design in the Monomail. "Okay, let's go after the passenger business," he said.

They rolled it back into the hangar and wasted no time getting the drawing back on the drawing board. The second Monomail, not yet finished, was

---

4. Harold Mansfield, *Vision* (New York: Duell, Sloan, Pearce, 1956), 96.

4-7 The Model 221 Monomail.

4-8 The Monomail in flight.

at a stage where modifications were still easy to make. Monteith and Egtvedt studied the available space and decided it was not large enough. They added 8 inches to the fuselage center section,[5] an innovation far ahead of its day, and put in six seats, ahead and below the cockpit, leaving room for 750 pounds of mail. This plane flew on August 18, 1930.[6] They called it the Model 221 (Figs. 4-7 and 4-8).

5. Kenn C. Rust, ''Early airliners,'' Chapter 5, *American Aviation Historical Society Journal* (Summer 1986): 121.

6. Peter Bowers *Boeing Aircraft Since 1916* (New York: Funk & Wagnalls, 1968), 30.

4-9 The XP-9 Model 96. The position of the wing on top of the fuselage was a handicap to the pilot. The structural features of this type were to prove valuable when Boeing manufactured the Monomail.

The modification proved inadequate so they stretched it another 27 inches, put in two more seats, and called this design the Model 221-A. When this design worked, Boeing converted the Model 200 to an eight-passenger ship.[7] The two planes went to United Air Lines, under the logo of National Air Transport, who used them on the Cheyenne-Chicago route.

The 221 was fast, but as Henry Ford had learned, so would Boeing: speed was not enough. Comfort was another primary consideration. The cramped and narrow bulletlike fuselage was uncomfortable for the passengers. The conditions bordered on claustrophobic. The external diameter of the passenger cabin was only about five feet. The passengers voiced their displeasure with the airplane, and Boeing went back to the drawing board.

The 221 design was significant. It employed countersunk rivets to reduce drag, and a monocoque construction. A smooth duralumin skin covered the wings, tail, and fuselage. The monocoque design permitted airplanes to become more efficient as they grew larger. The 221 was, without a doubt, the forerunner of today's large airliners.

The Boeing Monomail was the company's first commercial effort in this direction. There is no doubt that experience in the design and construction

7. Ibid, 121.

of the all-metal high-wing pursuit plane, the XP-9, was a factor (Fig. 4-9).

The single XP-9, commonly known as the Model 96, was significant in the Boeing story because the engineers applied the same technology to the Boeing 247. The Model 96 should have flown before the Monomail, but since it was Boeing's first monoplane to start through the factory, the design slowed production.[8] The construction of the XP-9 was new to Boeing, and the Monomail drew heavily on the experience of the XP-9.

---

8. Peter M. Bowers, *Boeing Aircraft Since 1916* (New York: Fund & Wagnalls, 1968), 173.

5

Air transport revolution

On March 31, 1931, there were rain showers southwest of Bazaar, Kansas. Visibility was poor under a canopy of clouds. John Blackburn was feeding his livestock in a field when he heard the drone of motors overhead. Suddenly, the drone became a sputtering, and through a break in the clouds, he saw an airplane with one wing missing, cartwheeling toward earth. The plane hit the ground with a sickening crash. There was no fire or explosion, but when Blackburn arrived at the site, he found the seven passengers dead. The impact of the crash buried one engine more than two feet in the muddy field. A moment later, the missing wing came floating to earth, landing about one-quarter mile from the main wreckage.

The crash set off a wave of public outrage. Knute Rockne, a national hero and coach of the Notre Dame football team, was dead in the wreckage of a Fokker F-10A.

After the Rockne crash, the U.S. Commerce Department grounded all 33 F-10As of T&WA, Pan American Airways, American Airways, and other airlines pending the results of an investigation. Investigators learned the wing root had rotted away, causing the wing to break off when the pilot tried to climb above the turbulence. The superior craftsmanship of Fokker's planes had been taken for granted, and there were no provisions in the design for inspection of critical areas of the plane. The wing root was inaccessible, even for repair.[1]

The Commerce Department instructed Fokker to reinspect all wings on his planes at specific intervals. This meant removing panels of plywood to get

---

1. *Boeing News* (February 1933).

at the internal spars and ribs. This was an expensive proposition for the airlines.

After the crash, the airlines also experienced a dramatic drop in passenger volume. There was no doubt the Rockne crash had caused the public to lose confidence in commercial aviation.

The XB-9 bomber

In the Boeing plant, they were putting the finishing touches on the first of two company-financed bombers, the outgrowth of Egtvedt's trip to Europe (Figs. 5-1 and 5-2). The bomber design was revolutionary and had the outward appearances of a large Monomail. The wingspan was 20 feet greater, the rounded fuselage 10 feet longer, and the rudder identical with that of the Monomail.

The bomber had one major change over the standard bombers of the day. It had two engines, mounted in the wings, a design that Henry Ford had tried and abandoned as impractical (Fig. 5-3). The engines, mounted in nacelles, protruded from the leading edge of the wings. This arrangement minir.iized the airflow interference between the propeller and the wing leading edge.

This engine-wing configuration was an aerodynamic breakthrough over the low-hung engines on the Fords and Fokkers. The new arrangement increased propeller efficiency and created a smoother flow of air over the wings. The bomber's gross weight was 13,600 lbs., and it was the biggest plane Boeing had built up to that time.

Another innovative idea introduced by Boeing on the XB-9 was the *servo tab*. This small, adjustable rudder built into the main rudder allowed the pilot to "trim" the aircraft without using the main controls. Other refinements, like retractable landing gear, differential rudder, and streamlined design, made the U.S. Army's biplane bombers obsolete almost overnight.

5-1 The XB-9.

The Boeing Company Archives

5-2 Two notable firsts for the Army are shown: the XP9-36, the Army's first monoplane fighter; and the Y1B-9A, the service test model of the Army's first all-metal cantilever monoplane bomber.

5-3 The big Ford 5-AT with engines built into the wings. The design, according to Ford records, proved no significant performance improvement, and Ford abandoned the design.

The XB-9 (Model 215) flew on April 13, 1931, and on April 29, Boeing test pilots Slim Lewis and Erik Nelson (one of the pilots on the record-setting round-the-world flight of the Douglas World Cruisers) set a cross-country record from Seattle, Washington, to Dayton, Ohio. The XB-9 averaged 158 miles per hour. Army Air Corps test pilots at Wright Field in Dayton flew the plane to a top speed of 185 miles per hour—faster than any pursuit plane in the sky.

There was great expectation of a sizeable production order for the XB-9 back in Seattle. That meant gearing up for a big plane assembly line. Meanwhile, the performance of the XB-9 introduced a new challenge. The bomber was faster than the pursuit planes for which Boeing was famous, and that meant coming up with a faster pursuit plane.

What happened next was ironic. Glenn Martin came into the picture again. Martin had designed a remarkably similar bomber called the XB-10 (Fig. 5-4). Apparently with the Army's blessing and funds, Martin had taken Boeing's twin-engined bomber idea, made a few improvements, and sold it to the Army. Martin won the production contract for bombardment aircraft, and Boeing got the leftovers, an order for seven XB-9 bombers. Boeing had missed the mark with the XB-9, although not by much. Industrial espionage was becoming an art, and Boeing had learned an expensive lesson in the value of secrecy.

5-4 Martin XB-10.

Next year's project: A new commercial design

William Boeing sat back to ponder his fate and that of his company. It was decision time: go back to designing and building pursuit aircraft or go out of business. Perhaps there was another course. If Boeing could revolutionize bombardment aviation, which there is no doubt the XB-9 did, maybe he could do the same for commercial air transportation. There was a need for safer airplanes—the Rockne accident made that clear.

The Rockne crash and the resulting public outcry almost shattered the infant air transport business. The planes had grown obsolescent to the point of sacrificing safety. Fokker's planes went back into service after inspection, but within a year the major airlines had scrapped them. The tragedy forced the existing airlines to seek bigger, better, and safer planes.

The death of Rockne started the first revolution in the air transport business. William Boeing was on the leading edge of this revolution, although that was not clear to anyone then.

The seeds of the Boeing 247

In August 1931, Phil Johnson asked his department heads for project recommendations for the coming year. This request landed on the desk of Fred Collins, an assistant sales manager. Collins happened to be in charge at the time because his chief, Erik Nelson, was on vacation.

During the XB-9's record-setting run across the country, a story leaked out that Boeing had designed a twin-engined transport plane similar to the new bomber on the drawing board. The rumor was not true, but Fred Collins began thinking about the idea.

Collins had been commuting between sales in the Boeing 80-A when he began to wonder. He was impatient and had some ideas.

Collins was also a pilot and during some of his flights he flew as copilot and talked to the flight crews. The responses to some of his questions were interesting. The pilots were no longer satisfied with the lumbering trimotor. Most of Boeing's pilots wanted a newer and faster trimotor, built like the Boeing 80 but sturdy looking like the "Tin Goose." They all, however, wanted an all-metal construction with a streamlined look, soundproofing, and high performance. There were many possibilities, seemingly limited only by the imagination.

When Collins arrived back in Seattle, he studied the completed B-9 and had an idea. He asked a simple question. "Why aren't we building a twin-engine monoplane transport like the twin-engine bomber?" Collins quickly answered his question, or at least he thought it did. "There must be some reason or someone would have thought of it by now."

He wasn't an engineer, he was a salesman, but the idea ate away at him. Of course there were safety factors that leaned toward trimotor construction (the extra engine), but as far as operating costs, nothing could measure up to a bimotor. Ford Tri-Motor cost about $225 an hour and the Army's twin-engine Keystone bomber, although slow, cost about $175 an hour.[2] Commercial air transportation was coming out of the dark ages, and operating costs were a primary consideration.

In response to Johnson's request, Collins prepared a 16-page recommendation for the study of a twin-engined, all-metal commercial transport. His recent commuting experience helped him gel his ideas.

Collins handed his recommendation to Phil Johnson, who in turn gave it to Charles Monteith. Monteith quickly assembled his staff. Collins's idea centered on the Boeing B-9 bomber idea, and Monteith's staff began substituting bomb load with payload. As his staff began developing weight and power ratios, Monteith began to think Collins was on to something.

Two weeks later, Monteith reported to Johnson, "We can build a twin-engine plane, but we'll have to concentrate on beefing up the engines. We calculate this plane will have a service ceiling on one engine of about 4,000 feet. If an engine failed along some routes like the Medicine Bow Range where there are 10,000-foot mountains, there would be a disaster."

Boeing, never one to be locked into one idea, had his engineers sketch other versions of the airliner of tomorrow. All the pieces needed for the future transport could be found in several contemporary Boeing airplanes. However, the pieces were not all incorporated into one aircraft. The Monomail, already off the drawing board and in the air, had many desirable features, and the XB-9 came close to having everything needed. Clair Egtvedt knew this, and so did Fred Collins. After reviewing Collins's recommendation, Boeing authorized expanded studies of a multiengine commercial transport.

Early considerations

On September 2, 1931, Boeing gave the go-ahead on what would eventually become the 247. Many designs began to appear on paper. One design was the Model 238. It was a high-wing trimotor, similar to the Ford but with a 90-foot span. (The Ford had a 74-foot span.) The three Pratt & Whitney 550-horsepower Hornet radial engines gave it a top speed of 165 miles per hour. It would carry 12 passengers and a crew of three.

Another design, the Model 239, was also a trimotored biplane and had

---

1. Mauno Salo, "The Crash of the Fokker F-10A," *AAHS Journal* (Fall 1983): 178.

an 85-foot span with a twin rudder arrangement. The three Hornet engines gave it a top speed of 152 miles per hour carrying 12 passengers and a crew of three. Both the 238 and the 239 would gross 20,000 lbs.[3]

A third design given consideration was the Model 243. This was a high-wing, twin-engine monoplane estimated to have a top speed of 169 miles per hour with two Pratt & Whitney 800-horsepower Hornets carrying nine passengers and a crew of three. It had a 90-foot span and would gross just over 18,000 lbs.[4]

The heads of the four airlines making up the United Airlines group had widely differing views on which of these designs would best replace the Boeing 80-A trimotor and other transports in service. D.B. Colger, vice president of Boeing Air Transport, saw advantages in a twin-engine design over a trimotor. Ed Lott of National Air Transport thought more effort should go into biplane designs. Colger and others also recommended studies using the proven Pratt & Whitney Wasp instead of the Hornet engine. Lott reviewed the Model 243 proposal and suggested that it had enough span and power to carry up to 16 passengers, thereby gaining an economic advantage.[5]

D.B. Colger liked the idea of using the more powerful Pratt & Whitney Hornet engine on the 243. Originally the Boeing team had wanted to build a transport weighing 16,000 lbs. and powered by two of the new Pratt & Whitney Hornet engines. However, the pilots of Boeing Air Transport, when shown the early specifications, flatly refused to accept the Hornet engines, stating that a 16,000-lb. airplane was too heavy and too powerful to land safely at some smaller airports. The design was, therefore, scaled down to 12,000 lbs. and fitted with Wasp engines. This decision would later prove to be a fatal mistake for the United Airlines group.

Go-ahead on the 247 design

In late 1931, Egtvedt, Johnson, and Monteith went to Boeing with their various proposals. After hours of debate and weighing of the facts, Boeing instructed Monteith to calculate the expected performance around Proposal #247, the outgrowth of Collins's idea.

The whole project was a bold one. By January 1932, when the engineering design had advanced to where informed decisions could be made, Nelson and Collins, led by Phil Johnson, took the drawing board 247 to United Airlines President Frederick Rentschler. In a bold bid for leadership of the U.S.

---

3. Victor Seeley, "Boeing's Pacesetting 247," *American Aviation Historical Society Journal* (Winter 1964): 240.

4. Ibid.

5. Ibid.

airline business, Rentschler placed an order for sixty Model 247s at a cost of over $4 million—a fantastic sum in those days and unprecedented for an aircraft that did not have a prototype flying. Only two Monomails and seven bombers had been built and flown, but the experience Boeing gained provided valuable technical confidence in deciding to go ahead on the 247 model

5-5 The Boeing 247 assembly line.

5-6 The Boeing 247s in the factory.

without a prototype. Rentschler felt confident enough to replace the United fleet with this yet unproven design.

United's board voted to purchase the aircraft, with the condition that its construction be secret, to get a jump on the competition. They did not want a repeat of the XB-9 fiasco. Boeing reviewed Monteith's calculations and by February 1, 1932, the Boeing team had started detailed engineering.

By placing such a large order, United tied up the facilities of the Seattle factory, thus ensuring that competitors could not operate 247s for at least two years. This move was to have repercussions when rival airlines began looking elsewhere. Production of this secret and radical passenger aircraft began on July 26, 1932 (Figs. 5-5 and 5-6).

The world's first modern commercial airliner

Seven months after Boeing had given the go-ahead to proceed with construction, the Boeing 247 was ready for its first flight. This was a remarkable achievement considering that the Seattle factory was small and the order for 60 transports was their biggest attempt at manufacturing to date. Boeing was still working on the P-12E and F4B-4 fighters when he took on the transport order.

At high noon, February 8, 1933, Boeing's chief test pilot, Les Tower, and copilot Lou Goldsmith taxied toward the takeoff point. Among those watching on the ground were Clair Egtvedt and Erik Nelson. Charles Monteith, chief engineer on the project, and the man responsible for its success, was in the plane as an observer, and William Boeing watched from his office window.[1] There was no publicity surrounding the first flight, and only a few hundred spectators saw the first flight of a machine destined to revolutionize air transportation in the United States.

The takeoff run was short and the transport lifted smoothly and steadily aloft. Fifteen minutes later it was over Puget Sound, and for almost 40 minutes Tower put the plane through its paces. He was getting the feel of the craft, and it flew perfectly (Fig. 6-1).

On a subsequent test flight several days later, the two pilots flew over Seattle for almost an hour.[2] Goldsmith cut the left engine. Not only did the

1. *Boeing News* (February 1933).
2. Ibid.

6-1 The Boeing 247 in flight over Seattle.

plane maintain level flight, but it climbed when he pulled back slightly on the controls. Tower's eyes sparkled; everything went perfectly.

The airliner that will put us in the Pullman business

The 247 was the answer to the teeth-rattling and dangerous Fords and Fokkers. The streamlined, stressed-skin, all-metal, twin-engine monoplane possessed some of the Boeing 80-A's creature comforts that were totally unheard of in the Ford Tri-Motor. The carpeted floors, reclining seats, steam heat, and a cabin insulated from weather and noise had led Boeing to say, "This plane is the airliner that will put us in the Pullman business."[3]

The Boeing 247 was an enigma. It was the same size as the big Ford 5-AT, but its shape only hinted at its performance. It was faster and there was no mistake about its heritage. Its bloodlines were obvious: it was the first cousin to the Monomail and sister to the XB-9 bomber.

Like the B-9 it had two Pratt & Whitney Wasp engines, each delivering 550 horsepower. At 5,000 feet with 75 percent power it cruised at 155 miles per hour, making it the fastest multiengine commercial transport plane in the world.

Up to that point, the Boeing 247 was the most radical passenger plane

---

3. Ibid.

The Boeing Company Archives

6-2 Inside a Boeing 247 during meal time. Notice that there wasn't much room in those days either.

design ever seen in the world. This airliner even looked fast. It introduced a list of "firsts" that would have all the other airlines awestruck.

The new Boeing was bristling with innovations, and it had vast improvements for the comfort of its passengers. The cabin was six feet high, richly appointed, and very comfortable by the airline standards of 1933.* The five seats on each side of the cabin (Fig. 6-2) allowed passengers to move freely in the roomy aisle, with one minor inconvenience. Because of the low-wing, cantilever design, the main wing spar ran through the cabin (Fig. 6-3).

There was a major improvement in the cabin environment. Passengers no longer suffered from the chilling temperatures they had endured in the Ford. The insulation served as a blanket that kept the passengers warm, and more importantly, served as soundproofing. Passengers could talk across the aisle in a normal conversational tone—a welcome relief for those used to the ear-splitting noise of the Fords and Fokkers. A major physical distinction of the Boeing was the matte-gray, sometimes patchy finish resulting from the anodic treatment of all external duralumin surfaces.

---

*Author's note: I was in the last airworthy 247 in 1981 and it was comfortable even by today's standards.

6-3 The wing spar was covered with leather, and the aisle-walker just stepped over the spar.

Pilot improvements

The 247's cockpit also maintained the high Boeing standard. It had dual controls and the main instrument panel had some 35 gauges and instruments—a vast improvement over the Ford (Figs. 6-4 and 6-5).[4]

The 247 was the first commercial multiengine aircraft to have a retractable landing gear, which increased speed by reducing drag. The gear was electrically or manually operated, and in an emergency the plane could land with the gear fully retracted since half the wheel extended beyond the wheel well. The low-wing designers said this would protect the passengers during an emergency landing.

The 247 also was the first aircraft to solve a major and often fatal problem: wing icing. On the leading edge of each wing, and on the elevators,

---

4. Dennis M. Powell, "The Boeing 248" *Air Pictorial* (July 1962): 195.

6-4 The 247 instrument panel was a bit more complicated that the Ford Tri-Motor's.

were pneumatic *deicing boots*, rubber edges that flexed when filled with compressed air and broke off the ice.

It was actually Boeing's brother-in-law, Thorp Hiscock, who invented the elusive deicer design. One day he was looking at a frozen flag and noticed that, when the wind blew, the ice fell off as the flag started to move in the wind. From this observation he thought that, if he could make an airplane's wing move, it too would shed the ice. After months of experimenting he hit on the answer. The deicer boot remained an industry standard until the electrical deicers came along.[5]

The appearance of trim tabs on the 247 was another first for a commercial airliner. Engineers had borrowed the idea from the servo tabs on the XB-9 bomber. These small moveable surfaces on the vertical and horizontal stabilizers used the aerodynamic force of the airstream to adjust the attitude of the plane. It was a welcome innovation for pilots. Until then, they had to

---

5. NASM files.

6-5 The Ford instrument panel.

maneuver the plane using the yoke and rudder pedals, a physically exhausting task.[6]

The 247 was an amazing aircraft by any standards. It weighed 6 tons, yet needed only 800 feet for takeoff and landed within 500 feet at a speed of only 58 miles per hour.[7] It could reach 10,000 feet in less than 10 minutes.

High-altitude deficiency

An early handicap the 247 had to overcome was its inability to take off fully loaded from a high-altitude airfield. Boeing called in Hamilton-Standard's chief engineer, Frank Caldwell, to work the problem. Caldwell started by

---

6. *Boeing News* (February 1933).

7. Joseph P. Juptner, *U.S. Civil Aircraft*, Vol. 5, 1931–1933 (Fallbrook, Calif.: Aero Publishers, 1974), 287.

adjusting the 247's fixed-pitch propellers to the best blade setting for takeoff. This solution proved satisfactory, even from high-altitude fields, but was still inefficient at cruising speeds. Caldwell then reset the blades to the best pitch for cruising. With a reduced load for takeoff, the plane performed perfectly. This problem was almost a duplicate of the Monomail problem, and Boeing would not settle again for a compromise.

After the demonstration, Caldwell showed Boeing his drawings of a controllable-pitch propeller design. After Boeing's engineers agreed that the design looked workable, Boeing told Caldwell to proceed with the manufacture of a prototype.

Probably the most significant feature of the 247 was its speed. Overnight it revolutionized coast-to-coast travel. The 247 cut travel time to 20 hours. That was a marked improvement over the Fords.

At 12:30 P.M. on July 11, 1933, a Boeing 247 took off from Newark Airport, New Jersey, on the first scheduled coast-to-coast flight. United's Captain Warren Williams landed the plane in San Francisco 20½ hours later, after seven stops en route.[8]

The Boeing's praises

After his inspection for Type Rating, the engineering inspector for the U.S. Department of Commerce said, "We are satisfied that, for performance, strength, and safety, this plane is a marvelous development and undoubtedly will prove one of the most outstanding contributions to air transport in 1933, and probably other years.

"In addition to the exceptional ratio of high speed to low landing speed, we found that the plane, fully loaded, would maintain level flight and maneuver well at the altitude required by the Department of Commerce with one motor functioning."

A higher compliment was paid to the new airliner when it appeared on the cover jacket of the Aircraft Yearbook for 1933. The covers of the April issues of both *Western Flying* and *Aero Digest* also featured pictures of the airliner.

As a stark contrast, only 30 years earlier, the original Wright Brothers "Flyer," which recorded man's first successful flight in a powered heavier-than-air machine, had a 12-horsepower engine, muslin covered wings, two propellers, and curved skids for a landing gear. On its initial flight it covered 120 feet in 12 seconds.

---

8. *Air Pictorial* (1962).

United's three-mile-a-minute airliner

The 247 was so modern it annihilated the competition. The 10-passenger airliner cost $68,000 and was worth every cent. Boeing estimated that the total operating costs were 2$\frac{1}{2}$ cents a mile. The 247 would make United Airlines the most popular airline in the world. United advertised the plane as the "Three-Mile-A-Minute Airliner."

At Seattle, Boeing's workers were working round the clock, and, by the end of June, had delivered 30 247s to United Airlines. Crew engineering, operations, and traffic training courses for the 247 went on for more than eight weeks.

In its first full month of service, the Boeing 247 brought United Airlines its largest-ever revenue in ticket sales. In Chicago alone, on a single day 160 passengers booked tickets at United Airlines, setting a new travel record for that city.[9]

Offshoot designs

Once the 247 became a reality, many suggested design modifications began to appear. Some even reached the point of having a design letter suffix assigned. None of these designs ever went beyond the drawing board, but together they showed the inherent versatility Boeing engineers thought the 247 had.

One model, a seaplane version with floats, had the capacity to carry nine passengers at 168 miles per hour. One drawback in this design was the increased weight. The floats would have decreased the payload of the aircraft by 1,500 lbs.

Another version was an amalgam of previous designs: a ski-equipped tri-motor with a twin tail and a swept wing. This monster would have had a top speed of 180 miles per hour.

One engineer, obviously thinking of the lucrative airmail runs, came up with the 247-B. This aircraft would have been a flying post office, with a crew of three and a mail clerk to sort and cancel the mail while in flight.

Another engineer, bowing to the idea that it was possible to sleep in comfort on a coast-to-coast flight, designed a 12-passenger sleeper. This 247-F had increased the gross weight to 16,876 lbs. and had grown a larger 77-foot wing. One can only speculate on later events if work had gone forward on this design.

---

9. *Boeing News* (June 1933): 2.

The public takes to the air

The summer of 1933 marked the greatest increase in speed in the history of air transportation to that point. From 1925 to 1927, the typical speed of a commercial airliner was 100 miles per hour. By 1932, it had increased to 115 miles per hour. With the introduction of the Boeing 247, the speed increased to 165 miles per hour. Each time the speed went up, so did the popularity of air travel.

The faster planes also brought an increase in night flying. The business community realized that night flying afforded a maximum time saving when measured in terms of a business day.

The speed of a plane depends chiefly on the shape of the plane, the materials used, and the efficiency of the power plant. It also depends on the creature comforts that add weight to the plane and influence its design. The flying public voiced its need for faster planes, but they also did not want to ride in the cramped space of a Ford or Fokker.

The engineers kept this in mind when they designed the Boeing. They allowed 170 pounds for each passenger and an additional 107 pounds per passenger for baggage, the seat, a laminated window, soundproofing, heat, and ventilation. The flight attendant (or in those days, stewardess) added another 19 pounds per passenger.

Boeing opted for a medium-sized plane, rather than the 30- to 40-passenger planes predicted by some. Boeing engineers felt that the medium-sized plane had the advantages of higher speeds, lower operating costs, and easier landings in case of an emergency. They also felt that a medium-sized plane provided operators with more flexible schedules. At a time when passengers were not exactly flocking to the airports, engineers felt that a large plane would make many trips only partially filled. With medium-sized planes, on the other hand, additional planes could be run as second sections if the traffic developed. Medium-sized planes could also be serviced faster and at less expense (Fig. 6-6).

The extra speed was another means of economy. The Boeing 247 flew farther per hour of flying time. Operations started on the San Francisco – New York route, with seven single-engine mailplanes. United Airlines used only three Boeing 247s on the coast-to-coast flight to carry the equivalent in mail.

With the new Boeing, it was possible for travelers to leave Seattle long after dinner time, be in Chicago the following day, and reach New York by dinner time that same night. Going westward, passengers could have lunch in New York, dinner in Chicago, and breakfast on the Pacific Coast.[10]

---

10. *Boeing News* (June 1933): 4.

6-6 Later Boeing bowed to demand by building the great ocean-hopping clippers like this Boeing 314.

Fuel consumption was another important consideration in an airline's operation. The Boeing consumed 360 gallons of gas per 1,000 miles, against a Ford's 675 gallons of gas.

The ultimate in air travel

The Boeing 247 was a giant step in the progress of American aviation. In 1933, it was the fastest and most modern airliner in the sky. It was the product of American technology at its best.

Americans felt that the Boeing 247 was the ultimate in air travel. Who could build anything faster or bigger and at such a price? An old mail pilot said that when it rolled out of the hangar on that cold February morning, "...No one will ever build a bigger aircraft."

The 247 made its first public appearance in a static display at the Chicago World's Fair "Century of Progress" in 1933. It was the symbol of man's progress in the twentieth century (Fig. 6-7). To the flying public, who had previously endured countless discomforts in noisy biplanes, the Boeing 247 was a "dream plane." At the Chicago World's Fair, the 247 sat in juxtaposition to a

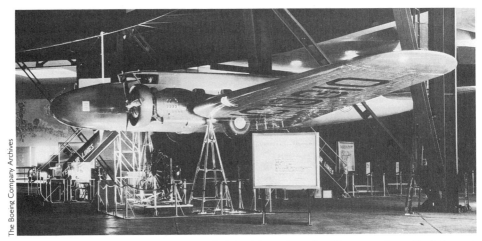

6-7 Static display at Chicago World's Fair. More than 4 million people walked the catwalk to get a closeup of the first modern airliner.

vintage 1915 plane to illustrate the progress in aircraft design and construction.[11]

Controllable-pitch propeller 247-D

The basic problem with the 247 was the high-altitude airport deficiency. Frank Caldwell solved this problem with the controllable-pitch propeller. Caldwell's propeller reduced the takeoff run by 20 percent, increased the rate of climb by 25 percent, and boosted the cruising speed by 5 percent.[12] The two-bladed propellers provided more blade area and reduced tip speed—tip speed was the culprit that produced annoying "propeller noise."

Long-cord NACA cowlings enclosed the upgraded 550-horsepower Pratt & Whitney Wasp S1H1-G radial engines. They helped reduce drag and improved the cruising speed. With additional fuel capacity the range of the Boeing increased to 840 miles. The earlier 247 was a three-mile-per-minute transport at its maximum speed; the new 247-D could set this same pace at three-quarter power.

The original fixed-pitch propeller Model 247 actually had a ceiling of 2,000 feet with one engine out.[13] The 247-D was able to maintain a ceiling 11,500 feet with gross load and one engine out—a substantial margin of safety in an emergency.

11. *Boeing News* (May 1933): 2.
12. Ibid, 1.
13. H.A. Taylor, "Boeing's Trend Setting 247," *Air Enthusiast* (Nine): 44.

The 247's increased speed allowed more attractive schedules from point to point, and reduced even further the flying time on a transcontinental flight.

Most of the changes in the 247-D were made for the sake of increased performance, but several improvements were for the passenger's convenience and comfort. There were some interior improvements, including a more efficient heating and ventilating system, a more practical lavatory, and more comfortable headrests for the reclining seats. Additional aids were installed to make piloting a little easier, too. Most 247-D models received a new back-sloping windshield. The Sperry autopilot and Goodrich deicer boots were optional.

Of the 75 247s built, 13 came off the line as "D" models, and nearly all the 247s were pulled from service at varying periods and converted to "D" models at the United Airlines overhaul base in Cheyenne, Wyoming.

More than a year had passed between the 247 and the 247-D. Aviation had taken giant strides in that year, but the 247 was not the high-stepper. The layout and structure of the 247 did, however, set for the next two decades the fashion for twin-engine transports (Figs. 6-8 and 6-9).

6-8   The Boeing 247 shown before its first flight.

6-9 In its heyday, the Boeing crowded all the other planes out. Shown are five Boeing 247s lined up at a midwestern airport.

7

The Airmail crisis

By 1934, in the depth of the Great Depression, Boeing was riding a wave of success. In just 18 years, his work force had grown to over 18,000, and he had produced 1,812 planes of 56 different types.[1] The Boeing 247 was the most popular commercial plane in the United States, and it was setting new speed records every week, flying 47,600 miles daily—the equivalent to more than 13 times around the world each week.[2] Donald Douglas had just rolled out the DC-1 (Fig. 7-1) and it showed promise, but for now the 247 was the sky queen (Fig. 7-2).

In anticipation of more and more profits from the burgeoning airmail business, TWA had ordered eight Gamma Type mailplanes. The American airline industry was maturing and beginning to make money. Airmail was still the chief source of the airline revenue, but more people were flying.

On February 9, 1934, the honeymoon ended between the government and the commercial airlines. Postmaster General James A. Farley, appointed under Franklin Roosevelt's "New Deal" administration, dropped a bomb on the airlines.

In a telegram to all the airlines holding airmail contracts with the U.S. Post Office, Farley said, "Pursuant to the authority vested in me by Section 3950, Revised Statutes of the United States, Act of June 8, 1872, and by virtue of the general powers of the Postmaster General, it is ordered that the following airmail contracts be annulled effective midnight Feb. 19, 1934."[3]

To make sure Farley covered all the bases, four telegrams landed on "Pat" Patterson's desk. In July 1933, Patterson had become president of

---

1. *Boeing News* (January 1934): 1.
2. *Boeing News* (November 1934).
3. Frank Taylor, *High Horizons* (New York: McGraw-Hill, 1962), 83.

7-1 The DC-1.

Harry Gann, McDonnell Douglas

7-2 The United/Boeing 247 and the route map in effect at the time of the airmail crisis.

Smithsonian Institution

NAT, BAT, PAT, and Varney Airlines when Phil Johnson, who headed these companies, resigned to become president of the holding company, United Aircraft and Transport.

The telegrams came as a shock to Patterson. Airmail revenue still accounted for 45 percent of the airline's income.[4] Patterson had a million-dollar decision to make. His choices were clear. One, he could stop flying entirely, as many smaller airlines would do, and lose the organization. He could also curtail operations by reducing schedules and eat away at the cash reserves. If he stopped flying, many employees would not find work elsewhere. United was the strongest airline in the industry, and keeping the employees on the payroll would show maturity and stability.

To Patterson the decision was clear. By the end of the first quarter, United was still flying but also more than $1 million in the red.[5] Later Patterson would say it was his first major decision as an airline executive. (Others have said that Patterson's first important decision came when he decided to hire female stewardesses four years earlier.) Some airlines—like Eastern Air Transport, TWA, and Pan American—also decided to keep flying and furloughed some employees. Others, like US Airways, suspended all service.

Patterson went to Washington to find out what had caused the administration to take such drastic action. It wasn't long before he peeled away the onion skin. Underneath was a teary-eyed tale of deception.

Patterson found Washington overrun with airline entrepreneurs. Some were operators who had lost their contracts, and others were spoilers looking to capture the contracts the former had lost. It didn't take long for the sour grapes to gather. Soon it was clear who did what; the question was "why?"

It was soon apparent to Patterson that the current problem went back to September 1933, when a special Senate committee headed by Hugo Black began investigating the steamship and airline postal subsidies. Ostensibly, the Black Committee was looking for corruption among the steamship companies. It was a sure way to attract headlines and public attention. They had no intention of delving into the airline subsidy.

One headline would do the trick. Roosevelt needed a public diversion, the "New Deal" programs like the National Recovery Act (NRA) were not delivering the people from the economic depression.

Spoils conference

Unfortunately, in an industry where stevedores were allegedly ruling with an iron fist and where blackmail and corruption were rampant, the Black Committee could find nothing wrong. Black was stymied and Roosevelt was nervous.

---

4. Ibid.
5. Ibid, 81.

Important congressional elections were coming up when suddenly up stepped a young Washington reporter, Fulton Lewis, Jr. In his travels, Lewis had heard grumbling from the small airline operators who had lost out on mail contracts. Lewis met Black one day and added some flavor to the allegations he had heard. Some of them suggested that the U.S. Post Office played favorites.

A gentlemen's agreement soon surfaced between Black and Lewis. "Give me a few heads and I'll give you some exclusive coverage," seemed to be what Black was saying.

Lewis drew a picture for Black of the small airlines like Braniff not fitting into former Postmaster General Brown's big picture. He pointed Black to a conference held in June 1930 and attended by some airline executives. Bingo! Black had the diversion that would eventually earn him a seat on the Supreme Court. It would also almost destroy the airline network the world had come to admire and copy.

The "Spoils Conference," as Lewis called it, was held in secret, or so Lewis claimed. Lewis alleged that there was collusion among those present to merge the airlines into groups that would financially benefit the attendees or their companies.

History now refutes those arguments, but in 1934, the historical perspective was too short. The conference of June 1930 was not a secret. The airline executives met in the Post Office Building. Papers like the *New York Times* began reporting on the meetings as early as May 19, 1930. Among those attending were Phil Johnson, Paul Henderson, Ray Ireland, and George Wheat, the UAT representatives. History shows that they were nothing more than observers. They attended the first meeting but not subsequent meetings.[6]

The United Airlines Companies were already merged into the airline network Brown was looking for. The collusion Black talked about was actually the formation of three transcontinental rivals who cut into the United Airlines market share and reduced United's airmail poundage by 40 percent.[7]

United also did not benefit from any route manipulations. It received a short route from Omaha, Nebraska, to Watertown, South Dakota, which it didn't want and later dropped. It also got a 100-mile extension of its West Coast route from Los Angeles to San Diego.[8]

Black's committee subpoenaed Phil Johnson and the other "Spoils Con-

---

6. Robert E. Johnson, *Airway One* (: Lakeside Press, 1974), 29.

7. Frank Taylor, *High Horizons* (New York: McGraw-Hill, 1962), 87.

8. Robert E. Johnson, *Airway One* (: Lakeside Press, 1974), 29.

ference" attendees. Their testimony was recorded, along with their objections to the assaults on their character and integrity. Johnson reminded Black that the mail rates and method of awarding contracts were consistent with the Watres Act, which by the way, he said, had been approved by a majority of both houses and by the present Democratic chairman of the Senate Committee on the Post Offices. Brown had also gotten a formal interpretation of his authority under the Watres Act from the Controller General.[9]

Johnson's testimony fell on deaf ears. Before Black was finished, more than 200 individuals and corporations went before his committee.

Black even called William Boeing to testify. Boeing testified that yes, he had made a lot of money on the stock transfers, which had taken place before any conference in Washington, and that the two were unrelated. Black accused him of making inordinate profits—more than $51 million over five years. Boeing countered that it was more like $12 million, actually. The $51 million was a paper profit and meant nothing unless the stocks were liquidated. Profits of that magnitude, he reminded the committee, were made by many industries during the bull years on Wall Street. It was a Bull-Market mentality that generated the profits, said Boeing, and not the manipulation of aviation or mail contracts.

Boeing had public opinion and most of the Republican Congress on his side, but in the long run it did little good. Just seven years earlier the Post Office had demanded a $.5 million bond from Boeing to fly the Chicago to San Francisco mail route. His opponents had called him financially irresponsible and said he would shatter the budding air transport business. Now he was accused of profiteering.

Black knew he was looking victory in the face if he played his hand right. Why, he asked, should the government subsidize the airlines when they were making huge profits and the country was in the depths of a depression?[10]

Former Postmaster General Brown testified before Black's committee. At Black's right hand throughout the hearings sat Fulton Lewis, Jr., writing question after question for Black to ask.

Paul Henderson's background included a one-time job as an assistant postmaster general. He attended the "Spoils Conference" and did not like Brown's style. He kept quiet at the time, but during the Black hearings told the senator so in private. This fueled the flames of the scandal and added another reason for Black's committee to avoid being confused by the facts.

At worst, the Black committee's investigation would have led to a revi-

9. NASM biographical files.
10. Ibid.

sion in the contracts and probably a new round of bidding. Instead, the result was the calamitous and deadly cancellation order.

The unexpected entry of the chief executive, Roosevelt himself, surprised everyone except Hugo Black and James Farley. Roosevelt's White House staff, ever alert on finding ways to discredit the Hoover administration, picked up quickly on the scandal being "uncovered" by Black's committee.

Roosevelt called Farley and Black to a secret White House meeting. Farley recommended canceling the contracts but allowing the operators to continue to fly the mail at reduced rates until new legislation passed through Congress. Roosevelt overruled Farley and Black sat quietly, agreeing with his chief executive. It was no skin off his nose, either way.

Richard Robbins, president of TWA, went to court to obtain a show-cause order why the annulment order should not be rescinded. That triggered the Attorney General to order the Justice Department to launch a criminal investigation. The pot was boiling. Brown even reported that someone was tampering with his private mail, but Roosevelt was confident.[11]

Call out the Army

Roosevelt called in his general of the Army Air Corps, Benjamin D. Foulois, and asked if his pilots could take over the airmail. With the Army Air Corps starved for appropriations in the Depression economy, Foulois saw a chance to win friends in the White House and on the the Hill. He could be ready in two weeks, he told his commander-in-chief.

Foulois's commitment was all Roosevelt needed to fan the flames. Roosevelt's subsequent actions would ricochet and become a national disaster.

One last effort to prevent chaos

On February 18, 1934, the day before TWA's mail contract expired, TWA's Jack Frye called Donald Douglas and asked if he could use the first DC-2 coming off the line. Douglas replied that none would be ready until April. Frye had an idea. He wanted to show that private operators could fly the mail more efficiently than the Army. He also wanted to showcase the new airplanes the airlines were pioneering.

Frye called Eddie Rickenbacker, vice president of Eastern Air Transport, and told him of his plan. Rickenbacker agreed to help. They loaded the DC-1 with as much mail as it would hold, and departed Glendale, California, for Newark, New Jersey.

Frye and Rickenbacker shivered and breathed oxygen bottles crossing

---

11. Ibid.

the Rockies at 14,000 feet. Over Ohio they ran into a storm and climbed to 19,500 feet, where they found an unexpected tailwind. They landed in Newark 13 hours, 4 minutes later, and set a cross-country speed record, beating the previous record by 5 hours.[12] One newspaper reported on the flight, saying that the DC-1 made all other air transport equipment obsolete in the United States and Europe. Frye and TWA had set the stage for a second air transportation revolution.

Meanwhile the Army Air Corps hurriedly modified a motley collection of bombers and pursuit planes, mainly open-cockpit biplanes. They tore out armament and extra seats, and converted bomb bays and cockpits into makeshift mail compartments. Most of the pilots lacked experience in bad weather and night flying, and many planes lacked landing lights, as well as illuminated cockpit instruments for nighttime navigation.

It was fortunate, in a sense, that the Army had scaled down the 26 mail routes flown by the private contractors to 14 routes. In hasty training before the formal operation began on February 19, three pilots died, during the week that actual flights began, vicious February storms swept across the country and added to the toll: two more fliers died, six were injured, and eight planes were destroyed. Eddie Rickenbacker called it legalized murder.[13]

By February 24, 1934, Army officers were stating publicly that they were facing an impossible task because of lack of training and equipment.[14] Farley was stating that the public would support him once all the facts were known.[15] The Army called out its reserve pilots but found that the Post Office did not have funding for the effort. They even tried to recruit the furloughed pilots from the airlines.

The editors of the *Seattle Times* criticized the administration's attack on what they saw as William Boeing's creation. Their editorial of February 22, 1934, said, "This is intended to advise Mr. Boeing, From Mr. and Mrs. Seattle, what his 'home folks' think about recent events including the government's hasty action in summarily canceling all airmail contracts.

"He (Boeing) took a chance when he piloted some of those early contraptions. He built machines and discarded them for better ones, all with the idea in mind that he was helping his country keep pace with the progress in foreign fields. He didn't try to sell stock to the public; he just 'plugged along,' backed by a handful of equally determined associates who shared his dreams and his ambitions.

12. *New York Times* (February 20, 1934): 16.
13. *New York Times* (February 18, 1934): 28.
14. *New York Times* (February 24, 1934): 6.
15. Ibid.

"Later on came United Aircraft, a brilliant combination of plane-manu-facturing, engine-fabrication, and transport operating companies. It was the backbone of the system of air travel and mail carriage which placed the United States first in all the world in this field.

"Seattle knows "Bill" Boeing intimately. It long has recognized him as a truly big man. The country is now realizing how big he really is as he sees achievements of a lifetime jeopardized, yet courteously declines to say a word in criticism of his government, its officials, or of the hasty service a devoted Army has sought to improvise.

"His 'home folks' are happy to express their appreciation of what he has done for Seattle, for his country, and for the science of aviation."[16]

By March 10, four more Army pilots had been killed, and Roosevelt had no choice but to order all airmail flying halted on routes that endangered pilots' lives.[17] This was another mistake. The public had grown used to fast-moving mail and when it stopped moving, they took matters into their own hands. They made up packages of letters and put them on as Air Express. At the other end of the run, the packages would be opened and the letters mailed locally. This seemed to be a clear violation of postal regulations and angered the red-faced Farley. As it turned out, the law did not bar the prac-tice.[18]

On March 12 Foulois ordered all Army planes grounded until a new schedule could be worked out. They didn't get back into the air until six days later.[19]

The public outcry was more than the administration expected. After a week without mailplanes, the president authorized only daytime flights of airmail. Two-day mail service was, however, a poor substitute for the pre-vious service, and the problem of dead airmail pilots didn't go away. The situ-ation escalated and the diversion Roosevelt wanted had backfired. The press was having a field day showing cartoons of Roosevelt and Farley leading a death march of deceased airmail pilots.

Roosevelt knew he had a crisis far worse than the failing New Deal. He finally gave in and took Farley's advice. He authorized the experienced airline operators to fly the mail until new legislation and contracts could be drafted.[20]

The airmail crisis had been a monumental blunder on Roosevelt's part

16. *Boeing News* (March 1933): 1.
17. *New York Times* (March 11, 1934): 1.
18. *New York Times* (March 20, 1934): 1.
19. *New York Times* (March 18, 1934): 1.
20. Ibid.

and now someone had to pay. General Foulois was looked upon as the one who had wrought havoc on the country and death on his pilots. There were some in Washington who wanted his hide. It didn't take long to find a skeleton in the closet. Foulois, it seems, had done exactly what the administration accused Brown, Boeing, and others of doing. He had purchased $7.5 million in warplanes from Northrop, Boeing, and Martin. Instead of using the bidding process, he engaged in "negotiations," a clear violation of the law. Once the mails were back in the hands of the private operators, the press and Congress went after Foulois, demanding no less than his resignation.

Aftermath

By the time new regulations were in place in May and the airlines were flying the mail again, a total of 12 Army pilots had fallen from the sky, and there had been 66 crashes.[21]

The airmail fiasco was not without a positive side. It proved that flying airmail was a job for trained specialists, not for Army pilots on a part-time basis. It also showed Congress that the Army's inventory of airplanes was woefully inadequate and that, as a group, the Army pilots needed better training.

Flying airmail was also expensive. It cost the government $2.21 a mile to fly the mail, but it cost the private operators only $.54 a mile.[22] That alone ended the perennial argument about who could fly the mail cheaper and more efficiently.

The New Deal offers a new deal

The once accused pirates of the American economy, the private airmail contractors, now became the heroes. Postmaster General James Farley called for new contract bidding, but that wasn't enough. Black convinced Roosevelt that Johnson and others conspired with Brown to parcel out contracts without competitive bidding and, therefore, illegally. The Black-McKellar Act also excluded from all airmail contracts for five years all airlines and the executives who went to the 1930 "Spoils Conference." As a result, certain individuals were persona non grata to the industry for five years. Anyone in the industry who hired Johnson or the other executives would also be excluded from mail contracts.

Phil Johnson was one of the individuals publicly banished from the air transport industry. Ironically, in 1930, Patterson was a junior officer in the

---

21. Roger E. Bilstein, *Flight in America* (Johns Hopkins University Press, 1984), 128.
22. Ibid.

corporation. He did not get an invitation to the meeting and was not affected.

Johnson bitterly gave up his presidency of United Aircraft and Transport and moved to Canada, where he went to work for the Dominion of Canada. While in exile, he formed Trans-Canada Airlines and went on to build it into Canada's premier airline.

The terms of the Black-McKellar Act excluded practically all the major airlines from the new contract bidding, so the airlines changed their names and reorganized under new officers. American Airways became American Airlines; Eastern Air Transport became Eastern Airlines, etc. Since the four carriers of United Airlines were individually banned from the new contract bids, United Airlines became the operating, as well as the management, company under the direction of Patterson on May 1, 1934.

The "new" airlines bid for their old routes, and in this fast shuffle, most of the original carriers won the new contracts on their old routes. Forty-five contract bids came into the U.S. Post Office, and Farley eventually awarded 15 contracts.[23]

Patterson bid $.38 an airplane mile on the old routes and won all but one of them back. The one he lost went to Tom Braniff, one of the more outspoken independents. Patterson's bid was less than one-fifth the Army's flying cost, and down from $.42 under the previous contract.

The legislation also dismantled the vertical holding company Boeing and Rentschler had built. United Aircraft and Transport split three ways. Boeing took over all manufacturing properties west of the Mississippi; Rentschler's UAT received all holdings in the eastern part of the country; and United Airlines became the operating company for what was still the largest air transport company in the country.

Aviation Corporation (AVCO) was the second company to break up. American Airlines found itself with C.R. Smith at the helm, who was able to position himself to make the most of the newfound independence. The third of the aviation giants, North American Aviation, which was controlled by General Motors, sold off $47\frac{1}{2}$ percent interest in TWA, and North American retreated permanently into the manufacturing part of the business. Most significant, Pan American Airways, which had representatives from all three aviation holding companies on its board, came through the crisis untouched.

The most significant offshoot of these events was the beginning of the end of vertical holding companies, in which big business controlled both manufacture and transport.

The New Deal's attempt to grab headlines worked, but it left many

---

23. *New York Times* (May 1, 1934): 7.

7-3 Boeing (middle), Johnson (right), and a man believed to be C.N. Monteith (left).

unanswered questions. Was there collusion in the awarding of mail contracts? Patterson believed Johnson and the others named in the conspiracy should be vindicated. Patterson went to the United States Court of Claims for breach of contract and out-of-pocket expenses totaling more than $2.8 million. Other attorneys added that the Fifth Amendment guarantees of due process were also violated.

The case dragged through the courts for seven years and during this time United Airlines remained in the New Deal doghouse. Finally, in 1943, Johnson, his colleagues, and Brown were exonerated of any wrongdoing and awarded a token $368,525. The Court of Claims said the contracts, "had been legally secured through open competitive bidding," rather than "through fraud, collusion or conspiracy." The conclusions the press drew were that the 12 Army pilots had died for nothing and that Johnson had spent five years in exile for offenses never committed.

In 1939 Johnson's self-imposed exile expired and he returned to the United States. Patterson immediately became president of the Boeing Company and Johnson took up his old post, remaining at the helm of Boeing and guiding the company through most of the turbulent war years. Johnson was instrumental in developing the B-17 bomber (Fig. 7-3).

The events surrounding the airmail crisis and the eventual outcome had profound and long-lasting implications for the American air traveler and the industry. After the dust had settled, the public looked at the airmail routes and could not help but notice that the original routes dictated by Brown in 1930 remained in place, and under the same airlines.

The system that paid the airlines $19.4 million in 1933 in subsidies paid out $12 million in 1934, and $8.8 million in 1935.[24] The Post Office even reduced the airmail rate from $.08 to $.06. The system that Brown had wanted had been hurried along by Farley; that is, to have airlines who primarily carried mail, carry passengers too. Only airlines that could make money carrying passengers could survive with the new reduced mail rates.

The Douglas transports that were about to climb into the skies would provide opportunities never before available to further Brown's vision (Figs. 7-4 and 7-5). The system the crisis had wrought remained in place for more than 40 years. In those years the airlines made money, and air travel became accepted as a normal way of traveling. Only when Congress deregulated the airlines in 1978 did a dramatic change in the airlines take place.

The Boeing Company Archives

7-4 At the time of the airmail crisis, the Boeing 40-B (right) had just about reached obsolescence, and the DC-2 was about to reach into the heavens, followed soon by the DC-3, the plane that would make all planes obsolete.

---

24. NASM files on the Post Office.

7-5 Soon after the airmail crisis, the Douglas DC-2 began flying passengers and mail.

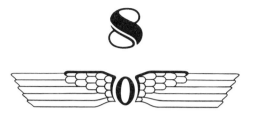

8

The London-Melbourne race

The 247's moment of glory came in the great London-to-Melbourne (Australia) Mac Robertson International Air Race. On October 20, 1934, the 11,323-mile race began. The race, actually two races run concurrently, spanned three continents. One race, the Handicap Race, measured an airplane's performance according to a formula involving such factors as gross weight, horsepower, wing area, and payload. The second race was a pure speed event with a minimum of restrictions.

Sir MacPherson Robertson was a 74-year-old Australian and a multimillionaire who was always looking for promotional opportunities. The London-to-Melbourne race was going to be his way to celebrate the 100th anniversary of the founding of Melbourne.

Air races in the early days were more than simply races for prize money. They were often the only way airplane builders could show off their products. The winning pilots would walk away with cash prizes, but the winning planes stood a good chance of walking away with orders.

In the speed race there were no time allowances, no restrictions about flying at night or refueling in the air, and no restrictions as far as fuel, engine size, and crew size. It was only necessary that the plane be certified airworthy, carry emergency equipment, and land and check in at five control points. The race crossed 16 countries with terrain ranging from deserts to long overwater hops, and from jungles to mountain peaks as high as 15,000 feet.

Twenty of the world's fastest planes had gathered to see which one would win the coveted gold cup, prize money, and prestige. Among them were Americans Jacqueline Cochran, flying one of the Granville brothers' Gee Bee Racers, and Roscoe Turner and Clyde Pangborn, flying the Boeing 247.

Turner had never flown an ocean before, but Pangborn had. Originally, Pangborn had planned to enter the race in the Granville Gee Bee "Q.E.D.," but problems at the factory made it look like he would never get to the race. Turner made him an offer to fly with him. Since the Gee Bee was still in the factory, Pangborn decided to take Turner's offer. He later transferred the Gee Bee to Jacqueline Cochran.

Turner and Pangborn were the only pilots in the race who had not previously flown the route. The Boeing was also new to the race and was thought to have barely a chance to finish. After all, an American transport plane up against the famous Gee Bee racer or the British Comet would surely get blown away.

Today the Boeing name is known worldwide, but in 1934 Boeing was known in the United States as a military plane maker, and was almost unknown in Europe. There was an advantage if they could make the right modifications to the airplane. The engineers at Boeing felt that larger fuel tanks would give the Boeing the advantage of staying in the air longer than the Douglas DC-2. Beating the Douglas, the only other American transport in the Boeing class, would have a real effect on the American air traveler's perception of the two planes. It was worth the gamble; what did they have to lose? The publicity would be priceless.

Both Boeing flyers were experienced pilots. Roscoe Turner (Fig. 8-1), a flamboyant pilot known for his moustache and personally designed uniforms, was the winner of the 1933 Bendix Air Race and the holder of the transcontinental speed record of 10 hours 2 minutes. Clyde Pangborn, a former Army flight instructor, was Turner's opposite—unassuming, quiet, and congenial. He was one of the few "round-the-world" pilots and the first to fly the Pacific Ocean nonstop.[1]

Turner said before the race, "I have chosen this plane because it has been in service and tried out longer than any other fast big plane on the market. It has proven its ability to stand up in regular day and night transport service. Speed is not the only requirement for the forthcoming race. Dependability has to be there too. This ship has both."[2]

---

1. *Boeing News* (Sept. 1934): 2.
2. Ibid.

8-1 Turner in his custom-tailored uniform before the race.

The Boeing Company Archives

The Boeing had left the factory registered as NR257Y and had the Boeing "Bug" emblem on the fin. So people would easily recognize the Boeing, they painted a large "5" on the rudder and a still larger "5" on the fuselage underside (Fig. 8-2). Turner's old race number "57" was on both sides of the nose and both sides of the aft fuselage. The port cowling eventually carried the name *Nip*, an American flag, and the phrase *Powered by Pratt & Whitney Wasp*. The starboard cowling had the name *Tuck*. After the race, the plane carried the map of the race with the words, *This plane carried the stars and stripes across the finishing line in the world's greatest air race* (Fig. 8-3).

Boeing modified the 247-D for the race by adding additional fuel tanks and increasing the fuel capacity to 1,125 gallons. Turner also had some of the airline-type radio equipment removed and replaced with his preferred radio equipment.

Jacqueline Cochran dropped out of the race when the Gee Bee "Q.E.D." (Latin for *quod erat demonstrandum*, quite easily done) proved not to be easy to fly. Of course, we know now that the Gee Bee violated some basic rules of aerodynamics, and its stall characteristics were unpredictable. Cochran said, "They were killers. Few pilots flew a Gee Bee and lived

The photo credit reads vertically: The Boeing Company Archives

8-2   The Boeing 247 before it had the more elaborate identification for the race.

The photo credit reads vertically: The Boeing Company Archives

8-3   The Boeing 247 in full dress after the race.

to talk about it. Jimmy Doolittle was one, and I was another."[3] Cochran's Gee Bee developed mechanical trouble and she quit the race in Romania.

The race wasn't easy for Turner and Pangborn either. Originally they were supposed to offload the plane in Plymouth, England, but because of bad weather they docked at Le Harve, France, where the French tried to make them pay an import duty of $20,000. They got around that but had to unload the plane and fly it back to England.[4]

As predicted, the British Comet won the race easily, but the Boeing finished the race in 92 hours, 22 minutes, 38 seconds,[5] following closely behind the KLM Douglas DC-2, which clocked in at 76 hours, 38 minutes, 12 seconds (Fig. 8-4).[6] K.D. Parmeinter and J.J. Moll, flying the DC-2, opted for the

3. Jacqueline Cochran and Maryann Bucknum Brinley, *Jackie Cochran: The Greatest Woman Pilot in Aviation History* (New York: Bantam Books, 1987), 108.

4. *Boeing News* (September 1934): 2.

5. *Boeing News* (November 1934): 1.

6. Ibid.

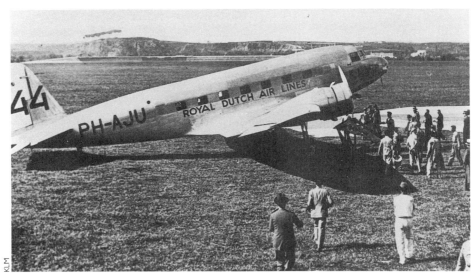

8-4 The winning DC-2.

first prize in the Handicap Race, and the Boeing took second place in the Speed Race. The DC-2 pilots earned $10,000, and Turner and Pangborn earned $7,500.[7]

More significant at the time, but not obvious to many, was the second best time in the race. The astonishing part was not only the time the DC-2 clocked, but the number of stops the airliner made. It flew its normal route, making 14 stops to take on and discharge passengers. At one point, it even turned back to pick up a passenger who had been left behind. The Douglas completed the race with three passengers and 421 pounds of mail. The Boeing made 10 stops. Had the KLM pilots opted for their rightful place time-wise, they would have drawn second prize in the Speed Race and only $7,500 in prize money.

Fate and skilled airmanship played heavily in the race. Bad weather developed along the race route, and the Boeing lost about three hours when it overshot Allahabad, India, by 200 miles. A heated finish developed when the DC-2 pilots were forced to land about 200 miles north of Melbourne. Turner and Pangborn raced out of Charleville, the last stop before the finish line, hoping to overtake the DC-2, but fate intervened. Engine trouble developed as the Boeing approached a required stop. Temporary repairs did not hold up, forcing Turner to land at Bourke, less than 200 miles from the finish line. They managed to get into the air again, but by that time the DC-2 had already landed in Melbourne.

---

7. Ibid.

Clair Egtvedt dispatched a telegram to Turner in Melbourne. "The boys are all proud of your outstanding accomplishment and fully appreciate what you and Pangborn have done by successfully completing so lengthy a flight over strange terrain. We also appreciate that you were flying a commercial transport plane where dependability was a first consideration in its design."[8]

Shockwaves around the world

Most of the world focused on the Comet and missed the importance of two American-made planes placing in the money. One astute British columnist did not. In the *London Morning Post*, of October 24, 1934, he said, "The results of the England-Australian air race has fallen like a bomb in the midst of British everyday commercial and military aviation. Preconceived ideas of the maximum speed limitations of the standard commercial aeroplane have been blown sky high. It has suddenly and vividly been brought home that, while the race has been a triumph for the British deHavilland Comet (the winner), British standard aeroplane development, both commercial and military, has been standing still while America now has in hundreds, standard commercial aeroplanes with a higher top speed than the fastest aeroplane in regular service in any squadron in the whole of the Royal Air Force."

Aftermath

A jubilant Turner and Pangborn and their Boeing 247-D left Melbourne for San Francisco on the steamer *Mariposa*. From there they flew from the Bay City to a hero's welcome in Seattle.

After the celebrations, the Boeing went back to the factory for conversion to an airliner. Turner delivered it to United Airlines in Chicago on January 2, 1935. The plane served United, still carrying the race map, until 1937 when United sold it to Western Airlines.

In 1939, the U.S. Department of Commerce (CAA) purchased the plane and changed the registration. It became known as "Adaptable Annie." They installed a variety of newly developed scientific instruments, including I.L.S., A.D.F., slope-line night approach system, airway marker system, stall-warning devices, and external lighting gear.

On July 17, 1953, Colonel Roscoe Turner made the last flight of the Boeing from Indianapolis to Washington D.C.'s National Airport. After a short ceremony, the CAA donated the plane to the National Aeronautical Museum at the Smithsonian Institution. Today it flies silently in the Great Hall of the National Air and Space Museum alongside its predecessor, the Ford Tri-Motor, and its successor, the Douglas DC-3 (Fig. 8-5).

---

8. Ibid.

8-5 The DC-3.

Boeing in
commercial service

United Airlines widely advertised the attractions of the Boeing 247 and, during its reign as a sky queen, greatly influenced the acceptance of commercial air travel. A UAL advertisement boasted that the 247 could reach an altitude of 27,500 feet above sea level—more than 5 miles above the earth. That was higher than any other large transport, but they went on to say, "However, United Airlines flies at a comfortable altitude, avoiding high-altitude flying except under unusual conditions."

They also boasted of the fuel economy. "Cruising at 62 1/2 percent of its rated power, it can fly 840 miles without refueling... ." That gave the 247 the longest range of any commercial aircraft and encouraged people who did not like the constant refueling stops to try the Boeing.[1]

The advertisements boasted of safety much like the Ford, but the Boeing delivered. An ad said, "At the end of the takeoff run, before the plane's wheels have left the ground, one of the engines can be shut down and the plane will climb, fully loaded, more than two miles with only one Wasp engine in operation."

What the advertisement did not say was that the copilot had to manually pump the fuel by using a wobble pump to gain full power on takeoff. It was also necessary to operate another pump to retract the wheels. (The electrical system was prone to malfunction at times.) This pump, like the fuel pump, was also located on the copilot's side.

---

1. Victor Seely, "Boeing's Pacesetting 247," *American Aviation Historical Society Journal* (Winter 1964): 268.

The copilot had other duties too. He had to make sure all the passengers were strapped comfortably into their seats. There is one story that a copilot didn't finish his cabin duties fast enough, and the pilot began his take-off roll. The copilot scrambled to his seat, strapped in, and began to pump the landing gear, instead of the fuel pump. The plane left the ground just as the landing gear began to retract, and one engine quit. The plane landed in the swamp at the end of the runway. So much for a one-engine takeoff. Fortunately, there were no injuries. The next morning they hauled the plane out of the mud, washed it off, and put new bearings in the engines. The plane resumed its flight with the same crew minus a passenger or two who decided to take the railroad.[2]

The 247 goes overseas

Initially the Boeing 247 had limited export overseas. The German Air Ministry purchased two planes on behalf of Deutsche Lufthansa. During the acceptance trials, the Lufthansa test pilot recommended improving the rudder efficiency and aileron control, and decreasing directional stability. The relationship between the rudder and the ailerons was not well known, and this suggestion was considered unusual at the time. Boeing made the changes, and it was to become typical in later low-wing monoplanes that the rudder became basically a yaw or antiyaw control.

Other comments by the Lufthansa test pilot included, "... the hand-operated landing gear retraction was too tiresome, and ... the seat belts were too short."[3]

After the test flight in January 1934, both airplanes were shipped to Hamburg. After seeing the new Boeing, the editor of the German newspaper *Lichterfelder Local Anzeiger* commented, "The Boeing 247's remarkable technical and constructive improvements make it one of the best airplanes built in the U.S.A."[4]

One of these 247s reportedly crashed in September 1939 while ferrying pilots during the invasion of Poland. Conflicting published information has the other Boeing scrapped in October 1936 or December 1937. Newspapers report that both 247s were in service on the Berlin-Moscow route up to September 1939.

---

2. Robert E. Johnson, *Airway One* (: Lakeside Press, 1974), 27.
3. Victor Seeley, "Boeing's Pacesetting 247," *American Aviation Historical Society Journal* (Winter 1964): 268.
4. *Boeing News* (April 1934): 1.

The flying lab

In the early years of United Airlines, it pioneered better navigation aids and radios for use in weather observation and recording (Fig. 9-1). The Boeing 247 became the tool for some technological breakthroughs in aviation (Fig. 9-2). One Boeing 247, nicknamed the "Flying Lab," began a series of radio static investigations. United engineers discovered that radio noise came mainly from static buildup and discharge from various parts of the airframe.

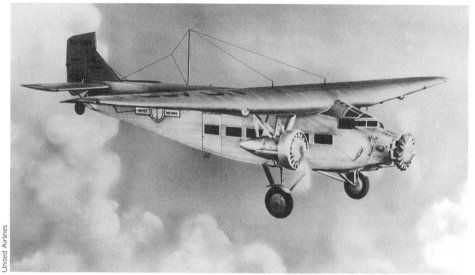

9-1 The United Airlines Ford Tri-Motor first used as a flying lab.

They had thought it came from charges in the atmosphere striking the antennas or airframe. The "Flying Lab" tested experimental radio equipment, altimeters, and landing system devices.

United used the "Flying Lab" until 1945, when they sold it to a subsidiary, LAMSA, in Mexico, LAMSA converted it back to an airliner, and it eventually flew into the sunset.

Soon after the appearance of the first "247 replacement," the Douglas DC-2, it became obvious that the 247's earning capacity and popularity would diminish. When the DC-3 lifted into the sky, the Boeing 247 lost most of its appeal (Fig. 9-3).

The end of the 247 signals a new beginning

In early 1936, United began thinning out its Boeing 247 fleet as the Douglas transports took over the main airways. It was logical to think that after

9-2 United Airlines's "Flying Lab."

9-3 The United DC-3.

136 The Boeing 247

United Airlines started retiring its Boeing 247s the aircraft would disappear from the commercial scene. One also would think that, since United no longer considered the 247 a viable profit maker, other airline owners would get the same message. The 247 seemed destined for a short-lived career.

On the highly competitive routes like New York to Seattle, the DC-3 outflew and outgrossed the Boeing. However, on the smaller, feeder routes where some airlines had a monopoly market, the Boeing fit the requirements perfectly.

During the growth of Western Air Express, General Motors had bought an interest in that airline. The 1934 airmail scandal delivered a nearly fatal blow to Western Air Express. To gain access to the new mail contract bidding, Western Air Express changed its name to General Airlines. It then purchased four brand new DC-2s for its new mail routes (Fig. 9-4). However, a second, nearly fatal blow struck, not long after the DC-2 purchase.

The Black-McKellar Act had forced General Motors and the other holding companies like UAT to divest their airline holdings. An offshoot of this divestiture was the sale of the brand new DC-2s. General changed its name again, this time to Western Airlines (WAL).

Western Airlines needed airplanes, so it went to United Airlines. Western's bid came at a timely moment, United was selling off its 247s and WAL bought four 247s to replace the DC-2s sold by General Airlines (Fig. 9-5).

Western continued to expand its fleet, buying and leasing more 247s and other aircraft. They operated a total of 33 Boeing 247s between 1934 and

Western Air Lines

9-4 The General Airlines DC-2. The tall Eddie Rickenbacker is pictured to the right of the logo.

9-5 Western Air Express's Boeing 247 at Great Falls, Montana.

1942. Nine were outright purchases, and the other 24 were leased for various periods from United Airlines.[5] Western Airlines would eventually build the second largest fleet of Boeing 247s ever assembled.

Some of the 247s came to Western as a result of the company's absorption of smaller airlines. In 1937, Western bought up National Parks Airlines and three 247s. Wyoming Air Service's first 247 came from United in May 1935. Wyoming became Inland Airlines in 1938 and joined Western in 1944 (Figs. 9-6 and 9-7).

As the DC-3 became the standard for airline travel, WAL also began replacing its 247 fleet. The 247 began to fade from the WAL fleet, but its useful commercial life had been extended almost ten years, thanks to a series of circumstances.

Those circumstances seemed to repeat themselves on a smaller scale after WAL sold off its 247s (Fig. 9-8). Small airlines like Pennsylvania Air Lines and Transport Company found productive uses for the now-aging 247. Many airplanes even migrated to Mexico and South America (Figs. 9-9 and 9-10).

Woodley Airways picked up two 247s and flew between Anchorage and Juneau, Alaska. Woodley reorganized as Pacific-Northern Airlines (PNA) and as late as 1964, PNA still operated two Boeing transports.[6]

Wien-Alaska Airlines also operated two Boeing 247s during the mid-1940s. One of the aircraft returned to Seattle in 1946 for modification. Addi-

---

5. Victor Seely, "Boeing's Pacesetting 247," *American Aviation Historical Society Journal* (Winter 1964), 239-271.

6. Ibid.

9-6 An Inland Air Lines Boeing 247.

9-7 Wyoming Air Service.

tional fuel cells were added in the outboard wings, increasing the range to nearly 1,200 miles. Earlier, Wien had fitted the Boeing with a large cargo door similar to the barn door on the DC-3.

Mr. Joseph Crosson purchased two C-73s (the Army designation) and ferried them to Alaska, where they continued to operate until about 1950, when they were scrapped. One of these aircraft had logged over 20,000 hours.

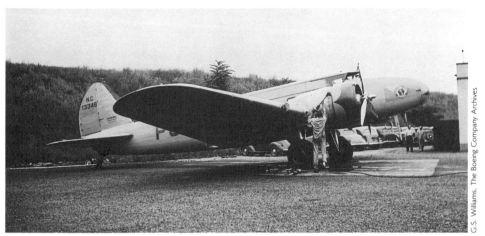

9-8 Pennsylvania Air Lines.

9-9 *Nicolas de Federmann*. Avianca operated this and 11 other 247s between the mid-1930s and 1940s.

One Boeing was a standard 247-D; the other was modified to be a "sleeper." The aft passenger compartment, separated by the wing spar, contained four standard seats—two on each side of the aircraft. The forward section, separated by a door, contained sleeping berths.

Military use

One Boeing 247 went to China in 1934. This 247, designated B-247Y, was used for at least two years by Marshal Hseueh Liang, Military Governor of Hupeh Province (Fig. 9-11).

9-10 Passengers pose while boarding an Avianca 247 flight in Colombia.

This aircraft was not unusual but what made it stand out was its speed. Test-flown in China on December 16, 1934, it proved unremarkable. It went on, however, to break many speed records in China. It averaged speeds of over 170 miles per hour on long runs and up to 200 miles per hour on shorter ones.

The phonetics of the English language are understandably difficult for some, and the word *Boeing* in China resulted in a new nickname for the 247. Boeing became *Bia-ying*, which translates to "White Eagle."

After a political coup in 1937, the "White Eagle" belonged to General Issimo Chiang Kai-shek. The Boeing flew until 1938, when a full-scale war with Japan saw it bombed to pieces while on the ground.

Early in 1942, 27 Boeing 247Ds were drafted into the military by the Transition Training Program of the United States Air Transport Command.

The Boeing Company Archives

9-11 The Boeing that went the China. The young marshall Huseen Liang is pictured in the middle. To his left is his American pilot, Julius Barr.

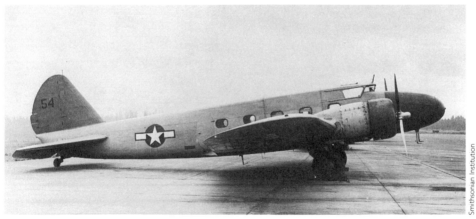

Smithsonian Institution

9-12 The military version of the Boeing 247, the C-73.

The Army called them C-73s (Fig. 9-12). To maintain spares and overhaul standardization, the Wasp engines were replaced by Pratt & Whitney R-1340s. They were used for transition training and cargo planes until the end of 1944.

At the end of the war, 18 went back into commercial service. The Army kept 4 as training aids and 4 were lost to hostile action. The Army also wrecked one while doing static wing loading. The craft withstood a 25 percent increased load over its design parameters. After the wings collapsed, the aircraft went to the scrap pile.

One military Boeing was different from all the others. It was the only 247 "bomber" and originally a United Airlines plane. To increase its range, it had four fuel tanks from Roscoe Turner's 247 inside the forward section of the fuselage. The aft compartment contained six standard seats (Fig. 9-13).

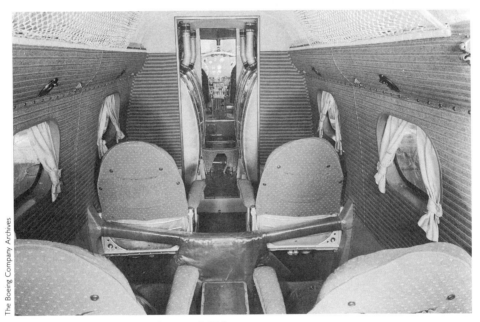

9-13 The interior of the Boeing 247Y.

The armament consisted of three .50-caliber Colt machine guns. Two were mounted in front in a fixed position to the cockpit on the nose, and were fired remotely from the cockpit (Fig. 9-14). The third, mounted in front of the tail, rotated and had a canopy for a separate gunner (Fig. 9-15). Each gun carried 150 pounds of ammunition.

All the modifications increased the airplane's gross weight by almost 2,600 pounds to 15,684. This 247 crashed into a mountain. It is not known if the crash was the result of hostile action.

9-14 The machine gun mount in the nose of the Boeing 247Y.

9-15 The rear gun station on the Boeing 247Y.

Boeing in foreign lands

The Canadian government's Department of Munitions bought eight Boeing airliners in 1940. A year later, they were sold or leased to several scheduled airlines in Canada. One was purchased by Maritime Central Airways and five were leased to Canadian Pacific Airlines for its subsidiaries. The Royal Canadian Air Force used one for spares, while the other went to Great Britain. The Royal Air Force used their 247 from 1942 through 1948 as a test vehicle for avionic systems.

The first Boeings used in Mexico were actually en route to Spain via the port of Veracruz. In March 1937, four 247s were in Veracruz on the way to the Spanish Republican government for use in the civil war with the Nationalists. To keep the aircraft from falling into the hands of the Nationalists, the Mexican government seized these aircraft as part payment of debts owed by Republican Spain to Mexico.

The four 247s were sold at auction, some to a broker who sold them to the Mexican airlines. Others found their way to Mexico in 1944 as the USAAF began releasing them. Records of the final disposition of most of these aircraft seem to have been lost.

Executive 247s

United Aircraft & Transport Corporation naturally used a 247 as an executive transport (Fig. 9-16). This 247-A, the sole example of its type, differed from the 247 mainly in the power plants—two Pratt & Whitney Twin-Wasp Jrs.— nacelle details, and the fuselage interior. The cowling was lengthened for the twin-row engine, and new intakes were added on the nacelles. Extra fuel

9-16   The United Aircraft and Transport Executive model 247.

9-17 ''California or Bust'' was written on the nose of this aging 247 owned by Zig Zag Airways.

9-18 The interior of the Phillips Petroleum 247-D.

tanks boosted fuel capacity. Other modifications included a special ventilation system, radio antennas, and 247-D fin and rudder revisions. UAT also used it as a Pratt & Whitney engine test bed.

United aircraft and Transport's *Bee Hive* Spring 1947 issue ran a story entitled "A Requiem for Old 247" as its 247 went to the scrap pile (Fig. 9-17). One pilot expressed his attitude about the plane. "That airplane had no bad flying characteristics. You could land her on dime, and get out of fields not much larger. We always asked for the Boeing when we had a tough job to do."

A third 247-D, earmarked for Lufthansa, completed flight trials in September 1934 and was ready for delivery when the order was canceled. Boeing stored the aircraft until Phillips Petroleum bought it in 1935.

Phillips had the plane modified to suit his style. He installed a plush interior with six seats and luxury furnishings like a radio, telephone, writing desk, and refrigerator. It also had long-range tanks and more powerful engines (Fig. 9-18).

10

The legacy
of the Boeing

When the Boeing appeared at the Chicago World's Fair, it symbolized what man could do with technology. The Boeing was also the victim of what it symbolized. It provided too much progress too quickly. It forced the creation of bigger and faster planes to further progress. The 247 gave the public a taste of speed combined with comfort, and they wanted more.

The Boeing 247 might have continued on the leading edge of the industry had it not been for two mistakes.

After the Airmail Crisis in 1934, William Boeing retired. Fred Rentschler took the helm and was faced with an immediate problem. The Boeing 247 generated excitement in America. It had captured the heart of America and everyone wanted to fly in one. TWA had been using the Ford Tri-Motor and saw the impact of the Boeing 247 on its revenue. So they went to Boeing for help.

Jack Frye, president of Transcontinental & Western Air, attempted to place an order for the 247 after the first 20 Boeings had been delivered to United Airlines. United Aircraft and Transport had other ideas, however. It agreed to a contract with TWA but only after it filled United's order for 60 planes. TWA couldn't wait.

Frye then approached Donald Douglas, owner of a small factory in Santa Monica, California, with a request. The result was the DC-1, which Douglas introduced on June 22, 1933. The DC-1 was eye-opening. Douglas had applied to even better advantage the formula pioneered by Boeing. The DC-

The Boeing Company Archives

10-1 Today the last survivors of William Boeing's Model 247 are residing peacefully in museums. This one is in The Museum of Flight in Seattle.

I quickly led to the DC-2, which Douglas delivered to TWA on May 14, 1934. It carried 14 passengers, compared with the 247's 10, and its cruising speed was 25 miles per hour faster than the Boeing.

Boeing's first mistake was allowing TWA to look elsewhere. What Douglas produced for TWA evolved into the plane that changed the world. It would outfly and outlive the Boeing 247.

The second mistake Boeing made was in the basic design of the 247. Part of the blame could be placed on the BAT pilots, who had rejected the original design of the 16,000-lb. plane powered by the Hornet engines. Boeing decided instead to use the reliable Wasp engine. This decrease in power made it necessary to cut the passenger capacity to 10.

Unknowingly, when Boeing scaled down the 247 the airplane became no serious match for the DC-3. Nothing they did to the 247 was enough to keep up with the Douglas. This was a costly lesson that Boeing never forgot (Fig. 10-1).

The 247 pioneered modern air travel and suddenly found itself outmoded in less than a year. What had happened?

Boeing anticipated what TWA was doing. They knew that something better than the DC-1 was due any day, and the DC-1 wasn't bad for Douglas's first real attempt at a commercial airliner. In a valiant but fruitless effort to keep up with the competition, Boeing produced the 247 "D" model. These aircraft cut the coast-to-coast time to 16 hours. On April 29, 1934, the first of ten 247-Ds went into service with United. United then spent $1 million to convert the old fleet to "D" standard.

The Boeing's structural integrity

Air safety continued to improve, but at a price. No aircraft manufacturer was immune. Between 1933 and 1939, ten Boeing 247s fell from the skies in fatal accidents.

The Boeing 247 was, however, a structurally and mechanically sound aircraft. On October 10, 1933, a Chicago-bound Boeing 247 crashed in Indiana, killing all seven occupants. Investigation revealed that the aircraft had not been at fault. The accident was caused by an item of "dangerous cargo" (a bomb) loaded in the freight compartment.

There has never been a case of a Boeing 247 crashing because of a structural failure. Most of the accidents usually involved collisions with high ground.

The 247 falls behind

United made great efforts to win more passengers over to its improved 247-Ds—efforts that included such innovations as New York – Chicago flights every hour in an already busy market area. The ploy didn't work. There was intense competition with TWA and American, whose DC-2s took only 4¼ hours nonstop, compared with the slower Boeing, which had to refuel at Cleveland. More importantly, the DC-2s made profits for their owners, while the half-filled Boeings barely managed to break even.

The London to Melbourne race did not pan out exactly as Boeing had wanted, either. The DC-2's overall performance far exceeded the Boeing, and the strategy only set the Boeing farther behind.

Although the Boeing had only a short reign as a sky queen, it carried people out of the noisy trimotor era and set the pace for modern, economical, and comfortable air transportation. During its short reign, it succeeded in leaving a legacy that would make William Boeing proud. Although, Douglas's more epoch-making DC-1 appeared, just months after the 247's first flight, it should not obscure the debt owed to Boeing.

The Guggenheim Award

On the evening of June 20, 1934, Major E.E. Aldren, president of the Daniel Guggenheim Medal Fund, presented William E. Boeing with the sixth Daniel Guggenheim Medal. The announcement accompanying the award read:

> He deserves particular credit for the development of an outstanding aviation manufacturing and transport organization throughout the United States. It was his vision and willingness to spend his money that has resulted in the formation of one of the best manufacturing and transport organizations in the world.

Boeing, with his usual reticence, tailored his remarks to be short but adequate for the occasion. "Now that I am retiring from active service, aircraft manufacturing, and air transportation, to be so greatly honored as to be recipient of the Daniel Guggenheim Medal is a real climax in my life. As the past years devoted to aircraft activities have been filled with real romance, the many forward projects not in the making will continue to keep me on the sidelines as a keen and interested observer."[1]

Boeing had joined a small membership of elite aviation pioneers. The other Americans to win the coveted Guggenheim Award were Orville Wright and Jerome Clarke Hunsaker.

Boeing retires

When the government ordered the dissolution of the United combine, William Boeing resigned as chairman and sold his stock. For years he had lost money nursing the young business to adulthood. Now when he made money, he was somehow suspect. It outraged his sense of justice and left him hurt. He walked away from the industry he had pioneered and, except to serve as an advisor during World War II, he did not return.

His new freedom left him time to indulge, more than ever before, in his hobbies. Even there he avoided mediocrity. He spent much of his time aboard his yacht, *Taconite*, which was equipped with the latest scientific and mechanical devices that delighted him. He cruised and fished regularly the coastal waters of British Columbia and Southeast Alaska. There he would rendezvous with the pilot of his private plane, first a Boeing flying boat, later a Douglas Dolphin amphibian, and finally a Grumman Mallard. The planes often flew him, Mrs. Boeing, and young William Jr. to the remote inland lakes.

When Boeing bought the Douglas Dolphin in 1934 (Fig. 10-2), it was an obvious salute to his sometime rival, Donald Douglas. When he took delivery of the plane off the coast of Canada, he announced, "I want to see how she climbs." Settling into the copilot's seat, stopwatch in hand, he matched the altimeter against the timepiece as his personal pilot, Clayton Scott, climbed for several minutes with an open throttle. "She meets performance specifications," he said. "We'll keep her."

William Boeing paid tribute to Donald Douglas a second time in 1940, when he bought a Douglas DC-5 (Fig. 10-3). Boeing sold the plane at the outbreak of World War II, and it went to the Navy as a parachute training plane for the Marines.

---

1. From the Daniel Guggenheim Award.

10-2 The Douglas "Dolphin." The original owner, William Boeing, traded it back to Donald Douglas as part payment on a DC-5 "Rover."

10-3 The prototype DC-5 was sold to William Boeing. During World War II, this aircraft was acquired by the U.S. Navy and called an R3D-3.

In later years, Boeing devoted his time to raising thoroughbred horses and experimental farming. In 1942, he bought a 500-acre grass farm in the green bottomlands east of Seattle. He donated his estate in Seattle's exclusive Highlands district to the Children's Orthopedic Hospital and settled on the farm. There he remained the rest of his life, but not to rusticate in bucolic idleness.

He operated *Aldarra Farms* as a business, but not for the purpose of making money. He wanted to prove what could be done with land, as he had proven what could be done with aviation. He made Aldarra Farms a challenge. Under his guidance, the farm doubled in size. Woodlands became grasslands, and the grassland produced better than ever before. He purchased the best cattle of the Hereford breed in Wyoming, and in the process taught himself to be an expert judge of the breed. He built the first noncommercial grass-dehydrating plant and used the product to improve the cattle's diet. He is credited with having improved the beef stock throughout the Pacific Northwest.

On September 28, 1956, William E. Boeing passed away. He had remained, until the end, a perfectionist and an active participant in life.[2]

---

2. *Boeing Magazine* (November 1956).

Epilogue

id the Boeing 247 appear at the right time, or was it ahead of its time, and did it carry the seeds for its own short life? An even more compelling question: might the course of transportation history in the United States and perhaps the world been different if the 247 had not been built?

With 20—20 hindsight, it might seem that the Boeing airliner was perhaps premature considering the requirements and technical developments at the time. The 247 was overengineered, too small, and underpowered, and the 247-D arrived too late. But make no mistake, the 247 technology was like the change from wooden warships to steel (Figs. E-1 through E-3). It put aviation on a big-business scale (Figs. E-4 through E-6). What it lacked, however, and the lessons to be learned from it were not lost on Donald Douglas.

If Boeing had not designed such a competitive and innovative airplane, the DC-1 and DC-2 would certainly not have appeared when they did. To take it one more step, it is possible, as difficult as it might be to imagine, that without the Boeing 247, the incredible DC-3 might not have appeared at all (See Fig. E-7).

The history of an airplane is, of course, not complete without the people who helped shape the craft and participated in the history-making process. Featured in this book are the known heroes, William Boeing, et al. But what about the unknowns—those men and women who in the early days worked for as little as $.14 an hour and put in 50- to 60-hour weeks?

Clarence Weeks is nothing more than a name in a fading ledger. He doesn't even have a social security number by which we can trace his background. He appears on a ledger with a note that he made $.14 an hour and worked 58 hours the week of September 16, 1916. The ledger shows he earned the paltry sum of $8.12. The ledger also shows that there were no income taxes or other deductions taken out of this king's ransom.

E-1 United Airlines was the first airline to boast 100 million miles flown. It passed this point on June 17, 1936, and the plane credited with passing this milestone was a Boeing 247. Today that airplane resides in the National Aviation Museum in Ottawa, Canada.

E-2 Another survivor is in the National Air and Space Museum in Washington, D.C.

E-3 The last flying Boeing 247 flew out of Orlando, Florida, in 1981, bound for England, where today it sits in the British Museum of Science.

E-4 The first Boeing commercial jet, the 707 – 100, was first flown on December 29, 1957, some 40 years after the first Boeing plane, the B&W. This version carried 179 passengers and had sound suppressors on the rear of the engines.

E-5 The Boeing 720 series was developed as a short- to medium-range version of the 707 – 100 series. It was lighter and on June 30, 1960, when it received its ATC 4A-28, it was sporting newer engine cowlings. It soon moved over for the more efficient Boeing 727.

E-6 The Boeing 747 "Jumbo Jet" was a logical expansion of the Boeing 707 configuration to a greater size to permit more economical operation through the reduction in seat-per-mile or ton-per-mile operating costs. The original 747 could hold as many as 490 passengers and had a crew of 3. It also had as many as 33 cabin attendants, more than all the employees of the original Boeing Company.

E-7 Gone are the days when even the shadow of the Boeing 247 paints America's landscape.

E-8 William Boeing in his retirement years.

The Boeing Company Archives

Weeks shows up as the lowest-paid employee, and one must wonder what he did. It is obvious that William Boeing would not have anyone on his payroll who did not contribute, so was Weeks the one who cleaned up the wood chips after the skilled craftsmen were finished for the day, and did he go for their beer at lunchtime? In that regard, doesn't he deserve recognition in this story?

And what about Herb Munter? He shows up at $1.00 a day and he was paid $6.00 that week. It's not possible he flew every day, given the weather and the fragile planes' shaky reaction to almost any strong wind. Was he on retainer, available for when conditions were right?

Engineer Wong shows up on the ledger, too. He also made $1.00 a day. Knox Martin made $40 that week, but you have to remember he was hired by the Navy. J.C. Foley appears on the ledger with the sum of $36 against his name, but after all, he was one of the executives of Pacific Aero Products. It's also strange that Eugene Gott and William Boeing are missing from the ledger.

All of these people are gone now, along with the unknown women who sewed the fabric on the wings and who don't even show up on the payroll.

Were they the wives of the workmen, as was the case with Donald Douglas? One can only wonder.

The paths of all these people, except for William Boeing (Fig. 10-11), are gone from the landscape of history, but their contributions certainly deserve a spot in the history of the world's first modern commercial airplane, the Boeing 247.

Bibliography

Books

Allen, Oliver, E. *The Airline Builders*. Alexandria, Va.: Time-Life Books, 1981.

Batchelor, John and Christopher Chant. *Piston Engined Aircraft - Seventy Years of Transportation*. London: Phoebus Publ. Co. Ltd., 1980.

Bilstein, Roger E. *Flight In America 1900 – 1983*. Baltimore, Md.: Johns Hopkins University Press, 1984.

Bowers, Peter M. *Boeing Aircraft Since 1916*. New York: Funk & Wagnalls, 1968.

Cochran, Jacqueline and Maryann Brinley Bucknum. *Jackie Cochran: The Greatest Woman Pilot in Aviation History*. New York: Bantam Books, 1987.

Davies, R.E.G. *History of the World's Airliners*. Oxford, England: Oxford University Press, 1964.

_____.*Airliners of the United States Since 1914*. Washington D.C.: Smithsonian Institution Press, 1982.

Howard, Frank and Bill Gunston. *Conquest of the Air*. New York: Random House, 1972.

Ingells, Douglas. *747—The Story of the Super Jet*. Fallbrook, Calif: Aero Publishers, 1970.

Johnson, Robert, E. *Airway One*: Lakeside Press, 1974.

Juptner, Joseph P. *U.S. Civil Aircraft*, Vol. 5, 1931 – 1933. Fallbrook, Calif: Aero Publishers, 1974.

_____.*U.S. Civil Aircraft*, Vol. 6, 1933 – 1935. Fallbrook, Calif: Aero Publishers, 1974.

Kelley, Charles, Jr. *The Sky's The Limit: The History of an Airlines*. New York: Coward-McCann, 1963.

Lewis, W. David and Wesley Phillips Newton. *Delta—The History of an Airline*. Athens, Ga: University of Georgia Press, 1979.

Mansfield, Haro. *Vision: A Saga of the Sky*. New York: Duell, Sloan & Pearce, 1956.

Maynard, Crosby. *Flight Plan For Tomorrow*. Douglas Aircraft Publication, 1961.

NAT Bulletin Board #9 (September 14, 1928).

Rentschler, Frederick B. *An Account of Pratt and Whitney Aircraft Company: 1920—1950*. : United Technologies, 1950.

Serling, Robert. *Howard Hughes' Airline: An Informal History of TWA*. St. Martin's/Marek, 1983.

Solberg, Carl. *Conquest of the Skies*. New York: Little Brown Co., 1979.

Taylor, Frank. *High Horizons*. New York: McGraw-Hill, 1962.

United Airlines. *Corporate and Legal History of United Airlines and Its Predecessors and Subsidiaries, 1925—1945*. Chicago, Ill.: Twentieth Century Press, 1953.

Vecsey George and George Dade. *Getting Off the Ground*. New York: E.P. Hutton, 1979.

Weiss, David Ansel. *Saga of the Tin Goose*. New York: Crown Publishers, 1970.

Whitehouse, Arch. *The Sky's the Limit: A History of the U.S. Airlines*. New York: Macmillan Publishers, 1971.

Magazines

Boeing News Vol. V, No. 9 (September 1934).

Boeing News (July 1934).

Boeing Magazine (June 1947).

Boeing Magazine (November 1956).

Boeing Company "Pedigree of Champions—Boeing Since 1916" 4th ed., May 1977.

Bower, Peter. "The Fokker F-32." *AOPA Magazine* (June 1980): 149.

Dick, Ron. "The Schneider Trophy." *Air & Space Magazine* Vol. 3 No. 2 (June/July 1988).

Johnson, Philip G. "Recent Developments in Air Transport." *Aeronautical Engineering Research* (AER-51-26 1929).

Larkins, William T. "The Aircraft History of Western Airlines." *American Aviation Historical Society* (Spring 1976).

McCarthy, Dan B. "Prairie Queen—Last of the Vintage Airliners." *Air Classics*, Vol. 10, No. 1 (January 1974): 42.

Neville, John. "Ford Motor Company and American Aeronautical Development." *Aviation Magazine* Part VI (September 1, 1929).

Newland, John H. "Reincarnation 1966." *Boeing Magazine* (July 1966).

Phillips, Reynolds. "William Boeing." *Boeing Magazine* Vol. XXVI, No. 11 (November 1956).

Powell, Dennis M. "The Boeing 247-Pioneering An Airline Formula." *Air Pictorial* (July 1962): 194.

Rust, Kenn, C. "Early Airlines." Part I & II, *American Aviation Historical Society Journal* (Winter 1985): 260.

_____."Early Airlines." Chapter 3, *American Aviation Historical Society Journal* (Spring 1986): 58.

_____."Early Airlines." Chapter 5, *American Aviation Historical Society Journal* (Summer 1986): 106.

_____."Early Airlines." Chapter 7, *American Aviation Historical Society Journal* (Fall 1986): 162.

_____."Early Airlines." Chapter 9, *American Aviation Historical Society Journal* (Winter 1986): 288.

_____."Early Airlines." Chapter 10, *American Aviation Historical Society Journal* (Spring 1987): 2.

Seely, Victor. "Boeing's Pacesetting 247." *American Aviation Historical Society Journal* Vol. 9 No. 4 (Winter 1964): 239 – 271.

Salo, Mauno. "The Crash of the Fokker F-10A." *American Aviation Historical Society Journal* Vol. 28 No. 3/4 (Fall-Winter 1983).

Taylor, H.A. "Boeing's Trend Setting 247." *Air Enthusiast* Nine: 43 – 54.

White, L. "Out of the Doghouse." *The Saturday Evening Post* (November 15, 1941).

Williams, Edward D. "MacRobertson 247 to Be Restored By United." *The Vintage Airplane* Vol. 3, No. 4 (April 1975): 4.

Wood, Barbara and Leland S. Prior. "Walter T. Varney Air Mail Pioneer." *American Aviation Historical Society Journal* (Winter 1986): 264.

"America's Aircraft Builders & Their Products." *The Sportsman Pilot* (August 1929).

Beating the Odds The First Sixty Years of Western Airlines. Western Airlines, 1985.

"Australian Race Attracts Prominent Fliers." *Aero Digest* (May 1934): 23.

Newspapers

The Tacoma News, Tribune & Sunday Ledger (October 10, 1970).

Dayton Daily News (September 28, 1956).

Washington Post (April 26, 1956).
Seattle Star (October 15, 1920).
New York Times (February 20, 1934).
New York Times (February 24, 1934).
New York Times (March 11, 1934).
New York Times (March 20, 1934).
New York Times (March 18, 1934).
New York Times (May 1, 1934).

Other

Congressional Record, Seventy-third Congress 2nd Session (April 25-26, 1934).
Washington Law Review & State Bar Journal Vol. AAI, #3 (July 1946).
Who's Who in Commerce and Industry 1940 – 1941.
Who's Who in Commerce and Industry 1936.
Who's Who in America 1938: 348.

Index